D1249538

Midlife Women at Work

Midlife Women at Work

A Fifteen-Year Perspective

Edited by

Lois Banfill Shaw
Center for Human Resource Research
The Ohio State University

Lexington Books
D.C. Heath and Company/Lexington, Massachusetts/Toronto

This report was prepared under a contract with the Employment and Training Administration, U.S. Department of Labor, under the authority of the Job Training Partnership Act. Researchers undertaking such projects under government sponsorship are encouraged to express their own judgments. Interpretations or viewpoints stated in this report do not necessarily represent the official position or policy of the U.S. Department of Labor.

Library of Congress Cataloging-in-Publication Data

Midlife women at work.

Based on data from the National Longitudinal
Surveys of Labor Market Experience of Mature Women
begun in 1967 by the Ohio State University Center
for Human Resource Research.
  Includes index.
  1. Middle aged women—United States—Employment.
2. Women—Employment—United States—Longitudinal
studies. 3. Middle aged women—United States—Social
conditions. I. Shaw, Lois Banfill. II. Ohio State
University. Center for Human Resource Research.

Published simultaneously in Canada
Printed in the United States of America
International Standard Book Number: 0–669–13159–8
Library of Congress Catalog Card Number: 86–7490

The paper used in this publication meets the minimum requirements of
American National Standard for Information Sciences—Permanence of
Paper for Printed Library Materials, ANSI Z39.48–1984. ∞™

86 87 88 89 90 8 7 6 5 4 3 2 1

Contents

Figures and Tables

Figures

Tables

Acknowledgments

While retaining responsibility for opinions expressed and any limitations of the research reported in this book, the authors wish to acknowledge their debt to many individuals who have made this research possible. We especially thank Kezia Sproat and the editors at Lexington Books whose excellent editorial work has greatly improved the readability of the book, and Joyce S. Davenport and Sherry Stoneman, who provided quick and accurate typing of the various drafts of each chapter. We are grateful for the expert programming and technical assistance of the Center's computer staff. We are especially grateful to Carol Sheets, Stephen R. Milstead, Mary Ann Graessle and Michael Motto.

Our special thanks to go Dr. Howard Rosen of the Department of Labor, now retired, who initiated these surveys and looked out for their funding and integrity for fifteen years, and to Herb Parnes, who was project director from the beginning of the surveys to his retirement in 1979. We also thank Kenneth I. Wolpin, the current project director, Michael E. Borus, who directed the project from 1979 to 1983, and Ellen Sehgal, who was for many years the project liaison person at the Department of Labor. At the Bureau of the Census many people have been involved over the years in seeing that the interviewing process moved smoothly. We also appreciate the dedicated efforts of the many Census interviewers who have been instrumental in maintaining a remarkably high sample retention rate. Finally, we are indebted to our colleagues, Jody Crowley, Stephen M. Hills, Lisa Lynch, Stephen Mangum, Gilbert Nestel and Patricia Rhoton for reviewing earlier versions of these chapters and providing technical assistance when needed.

Midlife Women at Work

1
Introduction and Overview

Lois B. Shaw

T he studies in this book are based on data from the National Longitudinal Surveys of Labor Market Experience of Mature Women (NLS). These surveys were begun in 1967 by The Ohio State University Center for Human Resource Research under a contract with the Employment and Training Administration of the U.S. Department of Labor. The members of the sample who provided the information were selected to be representative of the almost 18 million women in the U.S. civilian noninstitutionalized population who in 1967 were between the ages of 30 and 44.

Description of the Surveys

Sample Design

The sample design, field work, and initial stages of data processing have been the responsibility of the U.S. Bureau of the Census under a separate contract with the Employment and Training Administration. The sample was drawn from 235 Primary Sampling Units (PSUs) by procedures analogous to those used in the Current Population Survey (CPS).[1] In order to provide sufficient numbers of observations for reliable racial comparisons, the sampling ratio for black women was between three and four times as high as that for white. Thus the sample of 5,083 women originally interviewed in 1967 comprised 3,606 whites, 1,390 blacks, and 87 women of other races. So that the researchers could make accurate population estimates, each respondent was assigned a sampling weight based on the reciprocal of the probability of falling into the sample. In addition to the difference in sampling weights between blacks and whites, there is some variation within each color group. Differences also reflect further adjustments in the weights to make the sample conform to the known distribution in 1967 of the U.S. civilian population

---

I wish to thank Scott Martin for his excellent assistance in preparing this chapter.

by residence, age, color, and sex. In subsequent years the weights were recalculated to adjust for attrition.[2]

After the initial interview in 1967, respondents were reinterviewed in 1969, 1971, and 1972; an abbreviated mailed survey was conducted in 1968. After 1972 personal interviews were conducted at five-year intervals (in 1977 and 1982), and shorter telephone interviews were conducted in 1974, 1976, 1979, and 1981. This book is based on data from interviews conducted over this fifteen-year period, 1967–1982. Information collected in a 1984 telephone interview is not yet available for analysis. A telephone interview is scheduled for 1986 and a personal interview for 1987. The interviewing process ordinarily begins in April and extends over a two- to three-month period. In 1982, however, the starting date was delayed, and interviews took place during July through September.

Attrition

In 1982 about 70 percent of the original sample remained in the survey: 2,532 whites, 959 blacks, and 51 women of other races. Of the 1,541 women in the original sample who were not interviewed in 1982, 238 had died, 1,061 refused to be interviewed at some point and were dropped from the sample, and the balance were not interviewed because they could not be located or because of a variety of other reasons.

In any longitudinal survey it is important to determine whether respondents who remain in the sample continue to be representative of the population being studied. One method of examining this question is to compare the characteristics of the remaining sample with those of other national samples. Another method is to see whether attrition from the sample can be predicted on the basis of characteristics of the original sample. From the results of a regression analysis of the factors affecting attrition, it appears that the 1982 white sample remains fairly representative of the original sample. Women who were married and had children at home in 1967 were slightly more likely to remain in the sample than were unmarried women and married women without children (complete results are shown in table 1A–1). White women who did not reside in a Standard Metropolitan Statistical Area (SMSA) in 1967 were also slightly overrepresented by 1982. Women with fewer than twelve years of schooling were more likely to leave the sample, and those with some college were slightly more likely to remain. However, NLS figures on education differ little from those obtained by the CPS. With data weighted to adjust for attrition in 1982, about 24 percent of white women in the NLS sample had not completed high school compared with 26 percent of women in the same age range interviewed by the CPS.[3] This discrepancy may be accounted for by the fact that the NLS figure counts women who had obtained a general equivalency diploma (GED) as having completed high school, whereas it is not certain how respondents in the CPS answered the question on highest grade completed if they had passed a high school equivalency examination rather than completing high school in the usual manner.[4] In any event, the two estimates are reasonably close.

The black sample may be less representative than the white sample. Attrition from the black sample was lower in the South (or, more accurately, among women living in the South in 1967) and among women who did not complete high school. It is possible therefore that the current black sample has on average a somewhat lower socioeconomic status than the general population of black women in this age range. Comparison with other data sources confirms that the black sample overrepresents southern black women. About 60 percent of the NLS sample resided in the South in 1982, compared with only 50 percent of black women aged 45–59 who were enumerated in the 1980 Census. A comparison of the weighted NLS sample with the CPS showed similar proportions who had not completed high school in 1982: 51 percent in the NLS compared with about 50 percent of black women in the same age in the CPS. An extensive analysis of attrition has shown that it is not a serious problem in the NLS.[5]

Plan of the Book

At their fifteenth-year interview in 1982, women in the NLS mature women's cohort were 45–59 years of age. As documented in earlier research (Shaw and O'Brien 1983), these women belong to a transitional generation, the first in which a majority have combined work outside the home with marriage and childbearing. Most of these women either left the labor force for a considerable period or worked intermittently while their children were young. The first four chapters of the book examine the consequences of past work, family, and educational experiences for this generation of women.

This introductory chapter provides an overview of the changes in these women's work and family roles and their attitudes toward these roles over the fifteen years from 1967 to 1982. Also described are the women's varied work patterns during this fifteen-year period and how these patterns are related to changes in wages and occupational status. Chapter 2 describes the timing of the first return to work after childbearing and the effects of this early work experience on the labor force participation of women when they reach their late forties. Chapter 3 looks at a different measure of work success, authority in the workplace, and shows the extent to which authority is related to past work experience and current family roles. Chapter 4 describes the significant amounts of education that women have undertaken after they have passed the conventional age for school attendance. Determinants of attending college at older ages and the relationship between college attendance and employment are also examined.

The next chapters look at influences on current employment and future economic prospects of middle-aged women. At this life-cycle stage some of the younger women still have children at home or attending college, but the majority have entered the postchildbearing years. With the difficulties of combining work and child rearing largely past, new influences on employment, such as health problems of the women and their husbands, are likely to become more important. Because the amount and kind of employment among women in their forties and fifties will help determine the economic status of elderly women in the future, it is important to learn what influences the work attachment of these women today. Chapter 5 examines how husbands' employment or disability affects the amount of paid employment undertaken by their wives. Effects of divorce and widowhood on the number of hours women work are also examined. Chapter 6 looks at reasons for labor market withdrawal at this age.

The risk of poverty in old age is much higher for unmarried women than for their married counterparts. Chapter 7 estimates the probabilities of remarriage for divorced women of various ages and examines the factors that influence remarriage. Women's increasing work attachment makes it likely that in the future more women will have acquired pensions, Social Security entitlements, and savings of their own, thus enhancing the economic well-being of elderly women, whether married or not. Chapter 8 describes pension eligibility and sources of income that women expect to have when they reach retirement age. The final topic considered is middle-aged women's plans for retirement and what influences these plans.

Changing Family Roles

Between 1967 and 1982 the percentage of the sample currently married fell from 86 percent to 74 percent. These figures conceal large differences among race and age groups in the sample. Racial differences are especially striking. About two-thirds of black women were married in 1967; by 1982 only slightly more than half were married. These figures show net changes only. Many of the women who were not married in 1967 had married or remarried by 1982, and some women who were married in 1967 had experienced divorce or widowhood followed by remarriage during those fifteen years. Chapter 7 examines these changes, and particularly the probabilities of remarriage, in greater detail.

Table 1–1 shows marital status changes by age and race. Here it can be seen that black-white differences are greatest among the youngest women in the sample. Among whites, the percentage of married women was virtually the same across age groups in 1967. By 1982 the oldest women were least likely to be married; this difference was due largely to the greater probability of widowhood among the older women.

Table 1–1
Marital Status in 1967 and 1982, by Age in 1982 and Race
(percentage)

	Aged 45–49		Aged 50–54		Aged 55–59	
	1967	*1982*	*1967*	*1982*	*1967*	*1982*
Black						
Married	62.1	48.5	67.1	52.6	70.1	52.8
Widowed	2.5	7.7	4.8	18.1	7.2	24.0
Divorced or separated	22.3	34.8	24.9	26.7	15.7	17.3
Single	13.0	8.9	3.2	2.6	7.1	5.9
Total	100.0	100.0	100.0	100.0	100.0	100.0
White[a]						
Married	88.5	80.3	89.2	78.3	87.9	71.8
Widowed	0.8	3.1	1.5	8.3	2.2	14.7
Divorced or separated	5.9	13.6	4.6	9.4	6.5	10.4
Single	4.8	3.0	4.7	4.0	3.5	3.1
Total	100.0	100.0	100.0	100.0	100.0	100.0

Note: Sample sizes: Blacks, ages 45–49, 305; 50–54, 317; 55–59, 325. Whites, ages 45–49, 840; 50–54, 827; 55–59, 897.
[a]Includes individuals whose race is "other."

A very different pattern can be seen among black women. In 1967 older black women were more likely to be married than younger women, largely because of the lower rate of divorce and separation in the older age group. By 1982 the percentage of women currently married was more nearly equal across ages, but the youngest group still had the lowest percentage married— slightly less than half. For black women the percentage divorced or separated was twice as high in the 45–49 age group as in the 55–59 age group. Since widowhood increases with age, the influences of divorce and separation versus widowhood tend to be nearly offsetting within the black sample in 1982. When comparisons are made of black and white women of the same age, these very large differences in marital status should be taken into account.

For a majority of the women in the NLS sample, the fifteen years of the interviews covered a life-cycle stage marked by decreasing child care responsibilities. In 1967 85 percent of the women had children under age 18 living at home, and nearly 40 percent had preschool children. By 1982 slightly over one-quarter had children under 18 and less than 1 percent had preschool children. The transitional life-cycle stages covered by the sample in 1982 is shown by the fact that about 45 percent of the youngest third of the sample

Table 1–2

Percentage of Women with One or More Dependents and Mean Number of Dependents, by Year and Respondent's Age

Age	1967	1972	1977	1982
Percentage with one or more dependents				
30–34	89.7			
35–39	91.4	91.5		
40–44	80.3	87.0	81.0	
45–49		69.1	68.0	64.2
50–54			43.6	46.2
55–59				24.3
Total	87.0	82.3	63.7	44.3
Mean number of dependents				
30–34	2.8			
35–39	2.8	2.8		
40–44	2.1	2.3	2.2	
45–49		1.5	1.5	1.3
50–54			.7	.8
55–59				.4
Total	2.5	2.2	1.4	.8

Note: Sample size, 3,500.

still had children under 18 at home, compared with less than 10 percent of the oldest third.

Although the majority of women no longer have children who require personal care, the percentage with financial responsibilities for dependents—whether spouse's children from a former marriage, children in college, or elderly parents—is considerably greater than the percentage of families with children under 18. About 44 percent of the sample still had at least one dependent in 1982, compared with only 26 percent with children under 18 in the home.

Table 1–2 summarizes the changes in dependency over the fifteen years of the interviews. About 91 percent of the youngest two cohorts in the sample had dependents in 1967; on average, each family had 2.8 dependents. By 1982 the percentages of the two youngest cohorts with dependents had declined to 64 and 46 percent and the average numbers of dependents to 1.3 and .8 per family, respectively. In 1967 about 80 percent of women in the oldest cohort had dependents, but by 1982 the percentage with dependents had fallen to less than one-quarter.

As the number of young children to be cared for declined, women's contribution to the family through paid employment increased. In some cases

Table 1–3
Percentage of Husbands Who Were Not Employed during Year Prior to 1982
Interview, by Wife's Work Status, Age, and Race

Age	Wife Worked	Neither Worked	Total, Husband Not Employed
Black			
45–49	11.6	7.4	19.0
50–54	16.9	16.3	33.2
55–59	18.9	19.1	38.0
Total	16.0	14.5	30.5
White			
45–49	3.2	3.2	6.4
50–54	5.9	5.2	11.1
55–59	11.4	15.1	26.9
Total	6.7	7.9	14.6

their contributions may help to offset income losses when husbands become disabled or retire. In 1967 only 4 percent of husbands in the sample were not employed at all in the previous year; by 1982 the percentage of husbands not employed had risen to 16. Not surprisingly the percentage of families in which the husband was not employed was greater among older women and blacks (table 1–3). After they reach their fifties, one-third of black women have husbands who did not work in the previous year, and in about half of these cases the wife was employed. In the entire sample, about 16 percent of black married women were earners when their husbands did not work, compared with only 7 percent of white married women. These figures point up the importance of wives' earnings in black families. In the entire sample, about 16 percent of black married women were earners when their husbands did not work, compared with only 7 percent of white married women. The percentage of white husbands who were not employed in the previous year increases markedly as wives reach their middle to late fifties; over one-quarter of these husbands were not employed, and in about 40 percent of these families, the wife continued to work.

In cases where the husband was not working and the wife was employed, her earnings constituted about 45 percent of total income in white families and 50 percent in black families. In contrast, in cases where husbands were full-time, year-round workers, black working wives contributed about one-third of total family income and white working wives about one-quarter.

In 1967 about 70 percent of black wives in the sample were employed at some time during the previous year, and those who were employed contributed about one-third of total family income. By 1982 only 60 percent were employed, but these employed wives contributed nearly 40 percent of total family income. Thus black women's earnings became more important in some families, while in other families they were no longer earners. In contrast the percentage of working wives in the white sample increased from 48 percent in 1967 to 60 percent in 1982, but the average contribution of working women was 29 percent in 1982, almost unchanged from 28 percent in 1967. Among unmarried women, 75 percent of the income of white women workers and 70 percent of that of black women came from their own earnings in 1982. Both groups had earned about 70 percent of their total family income in 1967.

Work Roles over Fifteen Years

As women's child care responsibilities decreased, more white women entered paid employment, contributing directly to family income rather than indirectly through unpaid work in the home. At the same time, the earnings of black working wives became more important for some families as a substantial number of black husbands left paid employment. The increasing work attachment for the entire sample can be seen by comparing the amount of employment in 1967 and 1982. At the time of the 1967 interview, 45 percent of the women in the sample had not been employed outside the home in the previous year, 18 percent had been employed for fewer than 39 weeks, and 37 percent had been employed for 39 weeks or more. By 1982 36 percent had not been employed in the previous year, 11 percent had worked fewer than 39 weeks, and 53 percent had worked 39 weeks or more.

This overall increase in work attachment conceals large differences by age and race. The youngest white women in the sample showed increases in work involvement in each of the five-year periods covered by the surveys (table 1–4). In contrast, the oldest group showed increased employment between 1967 and 1972, when they were moving from their early to late forties, then stable employment in the next five years, followed by declining employment as they moved into their late fifties. The three age groups of white women have followed similar employment-age profiles: employment increased up to their late forties, stabilized in their early fifties, and then began to decline. As they reached each age, however, the younger cohorts were working more than the older had worked.

Black women's work attachment does not show a clear trend over the fifteen years. Women in the youngest age group worked more as they moved through their thirties and into their early forties, followed by a decline in their late forties. The older groups showed declining attachment by their early fifties; thus declining attachment appears at earlier ages for black women than for white.

Table 1–4
Percentage of Women Who Worked 39 Weeks or More in Past Year, by Age, Year, and Race

Age	1967	1972	1977	1982
Black				
30–34	44.1			
35–39	53.3	52.6		
40–44	55.7	57.2	60.0	
45–49		58.2	53.2	56.7
50–54			56.4	54.0
55–59				44.3
Total	51.0	56.0	56.5	51.7
White				
30–34	29.6			
35–39	34.5	42.5		
40–44	41.1	48.8	53.9	
45–49		50.9	53.8	58.4
50–54			51.0	54.6
55–59				46.2
Total	35.2	47.6	52.8	52.9

Over the fifteen years of the surveys, black and white women in the sample became more similar in their propensity to work outside the home. In 1967 between 30 and 41 percent of white women had worked for 39 weeks or more in the previous year, whereas for black women the percentage ranged from about 45 to 56 percent. These differences gradually narrowed over the years until in 1982 the percentage of women working most of the year was nearly the same for the two groups. In fact, in 1982 slightly fewer black women than white had worked for 39 weeks or more, and the percentage of black women who did not work at all was slightly higher.

Over these fifteen years of changing family circumstances, women combined work and family roles in a great variety of ways. It is difficult to characterize in any simple way the many different patterns of employment that they followed. The method I have adopted is to divide the fifteen years into three five-year periods and score each period by the work experience in that period. Within each period, three categories of work experience are identified: a woman who worked for at least 26 weeks in each year is scored "W"; one who worked at some time during the five years but fewer than 26 weeks in one or more years is scored "P"; and one who did not work at all is labeled "O." These scores combined produce 27 possible work patterns, but patterns involving abrupt transitions between O and W are rarely observed.

Table 1–5 shows the frequencies of these patterns for the entire sample.

Table 1–5
Distribution of Work Patterns over Previous Fifteen Years
(percentage)

Continuous		Increasing		Intermediate		Decreasing		None	
WWW	21.3	PWW	12.0	PPP	8.3	POO	5.0	OOO	12.6
		PPW	5.8	WWP	4.7	PPO	4.4		
		OPW	3.3	OOP	4.0	OPO	2.2		
		WPW	1.8	PWP	3.5	WPO	2.0		
		OOW	0.4	WPP	2.8	WWO	0.4		
		POW	0.1	POP	1.9	WOO	0.1		
				OWP	0.1				
Total 21.3		23.7		28.0		14.5		12.6	

Notes: W: worked 26 weeks or more in all years of five-year period; P: worked fewer than 26 weeks in one or more years; O: did not work at all during five-year period.
Sample size, 3,368.

The most frequent pattern, represented by the fairly continuous worker, WWW, accounts for only about one-fifth of the sample. About 13 percent of the sample are found at the opposite extreme: those who were not employed at any time during the fifteen years. Almost as frequent is the PWW pattern, which probably represents labor market reentry. A variety of other patterns also show entry into the labor force or increasing attachment over the fifteen years; almost one-fourth of the sample exhibited one of these increasing attachment patterns. Another 15 percent of the sample did not work at all in the last five-year period and thus exhibited decreasing attachment. Many of these women had shown only partial attachment in the earlier periods; only 3 percent had shown strong attachment at an earlier five-year period.

The 28 percent of the sample in the intermediate group represent quite varied patterns (table 1–5). Some are probably long-term workers who retired during the last period; about 6 percent were not working at the time of the 1982 interview and did not plan to return to work in the future. Of the remaining 22 percent, a few may be entrants who may work more steadily in the future (for example, the OOP and OPP categories), but the majority appear to have exhibited substantial periods of irregular work over the entire fifteen years.

Table 1–6 shows the distribution of the major work patterns by marital status and race. The intermediate group has been subdivided into those who have left the labor force by 1982 and have no plans to return (labeled "intermediate, decreasing"); the rest of the group is labeled "intermediate, other." The white unmarried group shows the strongest labor force attachment and the white married group the least. Differences between married and unmarried black women are much smaller; married women are more likely to

Table 1–6
Work Patterns over Fifteen Years, by Race and Marital Status
(percentage)

	Black		White		
Pattern	Married	Unmarried	Married	Unmarried	Total
Continuous	25.8	27.4	17.2	31.9	21.3
Increasing	19.9	17.6	23.4	26.9	23.7
Intermediate, other	17.7	22.5	22.8	19.4	21.9
Intermediate, decreasing	6.1	6.5	6.8	3.9	6.1
Decreasing	20.5	16.2	15.8	8.2	14.5
None	10.0	9.9	13.9	9.7	12.6
Total	100.0	100.0	100.0	100.0	100.0
N	449	451	1,876	607	3,364

show decreasing attachment and unmarried women intermediate attachment, but other differences are minor.

The "decreasing" pattern is that in which the women have not been employed during the five years from 1977 to 1982. Measuring decreasing attachment in this way shows no group in which substantially more women had decreasing than increasing attachments. By adding in women who had intermediate but decreasing attachment, however, both groups of black women show a lessening of labor force attachment over the fifteen years, white married women were fairly evenly balanced between increasing and decreasing attachment, and white unmarried women showed much more increasing than decreasing attachment.

Table 1–7 shows the distribution of work patterns by age. Not surprisingly, the youngest group was most likely to be in the stage where work attachment was increasing, and the oldest group was most likely to show decreasing attachment. The oldest group had more women at both extremes; more women in it worked continuously, and more women had not worked at all. Irregular work patterns were most common among the youngest group, probably reflecting the effect of their having younger children and a greater potential for conflicts between work and family.

Changes in Occupations and Wages

Over the fifteen years of the interviews, the occupational distribution of workers in the sample changed markedly for black women but only moderately for white women (table 1–8). The most striking change for black women was the movement out of private household employment; in 1967

Table 1–7
Work Patterns over Fifteen Years, by Age in 1982
(percentage)

Pattern	Aged 45–49	Aged 50–54	Aged 55–59
Continuous	20.1	21.7	22.1
Increasing	27.3	24.6	19.3
Intermediate, other	28.1	21.0	17.0
Intermediate, decreasing	3.9	4.8	9.3
Decreasing	10.6	15.4	17.2
None	10.0	12.5	15.1
Total	100.0	100.0	100.0
N	1,082	1,090	1,161

Table 1–8
Occupation of Current or Last Job, 1967 and 1982, All Women Who Worked during the Previous Year, by Race
(percentage)

	Black		White	
	1967	1982	1967	1982
Professional	7.4	13.4	15.3	17.2
Managerial	1.5	2.5	5.5	9.5
Clerical	11.1	14.7	34.0	35.4
Sales	1.9	2.3	7.4	6.0
Blue collar	20.4	18.9	18.6	13.1
Private household	24.5	11.6	1.8	1.8
Service	28.0	35.0	14.2	15.1
Farm	5.2	1.7	3.4	1.9
Total	100.0	100.0	100.0	100.0
N	711	578	1,431	1,645

nearly one-quarter of those women who had worked in the previous year were employed as private household workers, as compared with only 12 percent in 1982. Many private household workers probably moved into other service employment, which showed large gains. Substantial gains in professional and clerical employment can also be seen for black women workers. The largest gain for white workers was in managerial employment, but small gains in professional and clerical employment occurred as well. During these years blue-collar jobs became a less important source of employment for white women workers.

A comparison of the occupations of women in the continuous worker category with other women workers in the two years shows that continuous workers, both black and white, were much more likely to be professional workers in 1967 than were other women workers at that date (table 1–9). Both continuous and other workers showed gains in professional employment over the period. Whites showed larger gains than blacks in managerial employment, and both continuous and other workers shared in these gains. Except for these gains at the upper end of the occupational scale, the four groups shown in table 1–9 experienced quite diverse occupational change. White continuous workers showed net gains in professional and managerial employment and losses in clerical and sales work, with little change in other categories. Black continuous workers gained in clerical as well as professional and managerial employment, and these gains were accompanied by substantial movement out of private household and blue-collar jobs.

Changes in the occupational distribution of continuous workers represent changes in the same group over time; the other workers in table 1–9 include some women working in both 1967 and 1982 with noncontinuous work histories between those two dates, but many more women were working at one date but not the other. Thus some of the gains in employment status in the "other" category represent replacement of older workers and those with the least incentive to remain at work by younger workers and those with greater potential for obtaining good jobs. Women in the "other" category of white workers, like black continuous workers, were more likely to be working in professional, managerial, or clerical jobs in 1982 than in 1967. A reduction in the percentage of blue-collar employment occurred for this group through blue-collar workers leaving the labor force or moving into other jobs. Less than 20 percent of black women in the "other" category were in white-collar jobs of any kind in 1967; by 1982 about one-quarter were found in white-collar jobs. The largest changes, however, were the decline in private household and farm employment and the increase in other service employment.

In order to explore further how work patterns are related to occupational change, table 1–10 shows occupations of the last job ever held as of the 1967 and 1982 interviews for women with each of the three work patterns. Among white women, those with increasing attachment made very large gains in professional and managerial employment but were still well behind continuous workers in 1982. The intermediate and decreasing attachment groups showed small increases in professional and managerial employment, declines in clerical and blue-collar employment, and large increases in employment in service and sales work. On balance, the occupational position of these groups had declined somewhat, at least at the time of the last job held.

Black women with increasing attachment had made gains in white-collar and blue-collar employment, and those with intermediate attachment had nevertheless gained considerably in professional and managerial employment. All groups showed decreases in private household and farm employment.

Table 1-9
Occupation of Current or Last Job, 1967 and 1982, All Women Who Worked during the Previous Year, by Work Pattern and Race
(percentage)

	Black				White			
	Continuous		All Other		Continuous		All Other	
	1967	1982	1967	1982	1967	1982	1967	1982
Professional	15.6	20.6	3.5	8.6	20.6	23.8	12.4	14.3
Managerial	2.1	3.9	1.2	1.6	6.7	10.3	4.8	9.1
Clerical	17.7	19.6	8.0	11.4	39.7	36.1	30.9	35.1
Sales	1.6	0.8	2.1	3.4	4.9	2.6	8.7	7.5
Blue collar	21.0	18.9	21.1	18.8	15.6	15.1	20.2	12.3
Private household	16.5	9.0	28.2	13.2	0.8	0.8	2.3	2.3
Service	25.3	26.3	29.2	40.7	10.1	10.0	16.4	17.3
Farm	0.2	1.0	7.6	2.3	1.6	1.2	4.4	2.2
Total	100.0	100.0	100.0	100.0	100.0	100.0	100.0	100.0
N	216	224	495	354	495	507	936	1,138

Table 1–10
Occupation of Current Job or Last Job Ever Held as of 1967 and 1982, by Work Pattern and Race
(percentage)

	Continuous		Increasing		Intermediate		Decreasing		None
	1967	1982	1967	1982	1967	1982	1967	1982	1967
Black									
Professional and managerial	18	24	6	8	4	10	4	2	0
Clerical	17	20	8	13	12	10	8	11	1
Blue collar[a]	22	19	21	24	18	16	23	25	11
Sales and service	26	27	32	41	33	39	22	32	28
Private household and farm	17	10	29	14	30	24	38	29	43
Never worked	0	0	4	0	3	0	5	0	18
Total	100	100	100	100	100	100	100	100	100
White									
Professional and managerial	27	34	17	26	16	18	10	12	10
Clerical	40	36	46	37	37	32	36	24	36
Blue collar[a]	16	15	14	12	16	15	22	20	18
Sales and service	14	13	18	21	23	28	21	32	18
Private household and farm	3	2	3	4	5	7	4	12	5
Never worked	0	0	2	0	3	0	6	0	13
Total	100	100	100	100	100	100	100	100	100

[a]Includes craftswomen, operatives, and laborers.
[b]Includes sales, private household and other service workers, and farm workers.

Probably the majority of these workers moved into other service employment or left the labor force. No black women whose last job in 1967 was professional or managerial stayed out of the labor force over the entire fifteen years.

In summary, table 1–10 shows that as of 1967, women who would be continuously employed over the next fifteen years were much more likely to be working in professional or managerial jobs (and for black women, clerical jobs) than were other women. While these continously employed women gained in occupational status over the fifteen years and remained in higher-status jobs than other women, other groups, especially those with increasing attachment, made even larger gains.

Real wages of black women wage and salary workers increased by about 23 percent between 1967 and 1982, while those of white women increased only 6 percent (table 1–11). Among continuous workers, the difference between the races was small; white women's wages increased about 18 percent and those of black women by about 20 percent. Among other workers, however, many of whom were employed at one date but not the other, black women employed in 1982 had wages 26 percent greater than those employed in 1967, whereas wages of white women employed in 1982 were no higher than those of women employed in 1967. These differences were probably due in part to the fact that black women in the lowest-paid positions, private household and farm laborer employment, moved into service or other better-paying jobs or left the labor force.

Almost all of the gains in real wages shown in table 1–11 were realized in the period between 1967 and 1972. White women who were continuous workers showed modest gains between 1972 and 1977, but the wages of other groups showed no increase. All groups showed losses of 3 to 4 percent between 1977 and 1982 as real wages failed to keep up with inflation.

Table 1–11
Mean Hourly Rate of Pay by Year, Work Pattern, and Race
(1982 dollars)

Year	1967	1972	1977	1982
Black				
All wage and salary workers	4.61	5.98	5.86	5.69
Continuous	5.45	6.85	6.87	6.57
All Other	4.13	5.41	5.22	5.07
White				
All wage and salary workers	6.01	6.56	6.60	6.37
Continuous	6.58	7.76	8.03	7.80
All Other	5.66	5.94	5.90	5.67

Attitudes toward Work and Women's Roles

The fifteen years of the NLS interviews spanned a period in which women's roles were the subject of a great deal of debate. Questions on attitudes toward women's roles asked in the NLS during these years document changing attitudes among middle-aged as well as younger women.

At five-year intervals three questions were asked on whether it is all right for a married woman with children to take a full-time job under three conditions: (1) if it is absolutely necessary to make ends meet; (2) if she wants to and her husband agrees; and (3) if she prefers to work, even if her husband does not particularly like the idea. In all years, close to 95 percent of the sample agreed that it was all right for a woman to work if it was necessary to make ends meet. In 1967 three-quarters of the sample thought it was all right for her to work if her husband agreed, and these percentages approving of work in this case increased to over 90 percent by 1982. The largest change occurred in the third case. In 1967 only 14 percent of the sample thought that it was all right for a woman to work if her husband did not want her to, but by 1982 44 percent of the sample approved of women working in such cases.

It is interesting to note the age differences in this changing view. Table 1–12 shows the percentage agreeing with statement 3 by age in each year. For purposes of comparison, the views of women from the younger NLS cohort are shown as well. In 1967 there appears to have been a broad social consensus across all age groups that women should not work unless their husbands agreed. By 1972 a somewhat smaller percentage of women thought that the husband's approval was necessary; the largest change in views was among women under age 40. Very large changes occurred between 1972 and 1977, especially among women in their twenties—a majority of whom by

Table 1–12
Percentage of Women Agreeing or Strongly Agreeing with the Statement, "It Is All Right for a Woman to Work If She Wants to, Even If Her Husband Doesn't Particularly Like the Idea," by Year and Age

Age	1967	1972	1977	1982
20–24[a]	13.6	23.7	—	—
25–29[a]	—	26.9	53.2	—
30–34	14.4	—	48.2[b]	—
35–39	14.3	23.7	—	—
40–44	13.0	20.6	36.3	—
45–49		19.5	32.2	50.4
50–54			29.3	44.7
55–59				37.7

[a]From NLS young women's sample in 1968, 1972, and 1978.
[b]From NLS young women's sample in 1978.

1977 agreed that it was all right for a woman to work without her husband's approval. In 1977 a very large gap is apparent between the views of younger and older women. We do not have data on these younger women's views in the 1980s, but older women have continued to move in the direction of younger women's views; in 1982 the 45–49 group was almost evenly divided in their views on the propriety of working regardless of a husband's approval. The age differentials in views expressed have continued to widen within the mature women's cohort.

Views on the propriety of women working have become considerably more favorable. How well do women like their own roles, both at home and at work? Table 1–13 shows the responses of the women to questions on how well they liked their jobs (if working) and housework (if married). In all groups except the youngest, the majority of women enjoyed both kinds of work very much in 1967, but jobs were viewed somewhat more favorably than housework. Between 1967 and 1982, satisfaction with jobs declined somewhat for the older two-thirds of working women in the sample and remained nearly constant for the younger women. Over the same period, satisfaction with housework declined for all groups, but the decline was greatest for the youngest women. As in the questions on role attitudes, these questions show the younger women to be less satisfied with traditional roles than the older women in the sample.

Although the percentage of working women who report liking their work is higher than the percentage of housewives who report a liking for housework, this comparison does not mean that women generally find jobs more enjoyable than housework. All but a small minority of women do housework to some extent, but some women do not hold jobs. Presumably some of those who do not work outside the home prefer doing housework to the kind of work they would do if employed, but these women's opinion of how well they would like the content of a potential job is not known.

Although we do not know how well full-time housewives might enjoy a job if they were to become employed, we can see whether employed married women and full-time housewives feel differently about housework. In 1967 for the sample as a whole, satisfaction with housework was not markedly different for employed women and full-time housewives (table 1–14). In the youngest and oldest age groups, employed women were slightly less satisfied with housework than women who were not employed, but in the middle group employed women were more satisfied than full-time housewives. In 1982, however, women who were full-time housewives were much more satisfied with housework than were women employed outside the home. Although satisfaction was somewhat lower among full-time housewives in 1982 as compared with 1967, the largest change was among employed women. In the youngest group especially, working women expressed much less satisfaction with housework in 1982 than in 1967; the difference between

Table 1-13
Working Women's Attitude toward Their Jobs and Married Women's Attitude toward Housework in 1967 and 1982, by Age in 1982
(percentage)

Attitude	Aged 45–49[a]		Aged 50–54[a]		Aged 55–59[a]		Total	
	1967	1982	1967	1982	1967	1982	1967	1982
Job								
Like very much	64.5	63.3	70.2	63.8	66.0	58.4	67.0	62.0
Like somewhat	31.5	31.0	25.5	32.1	29.1	33.8	28.6	32.2
Dislike	4.1	5.7	4.2	4.1	4.9	3.7	4.5	5.8
Total	100.0	100.0	100.0	100.0	100.0	100.0	100.0	100.0
N	502	719	568	644	630	571	1,700	1,934
Housework								
Like very much	49.2	35.2	53.2	43.0	53.7	42.2	52.1	40.2
Like somewhat	34.6	45.8	33.9	40.9	32.5	42.1	33.6	42.9
Dislike	16.1	19.0	12.9	16.1	13.8	15.6	14.3	16.9
Total	100.0	100.0	100.0	100.0	100.0	100.0	100.0	100.0
N	915	808	938	810	989	804	2,842	2,422

[a] Age in 1982.

Table 1–14
Married Women's Attitude toward Housework in 1967 and 1982, by Employment Status and Age
(*percentage*)

Attitude	Aged 45–49[a]		Aged 50–54[a]		Aged 55–59[a]		Total	
	1967	1982	1967	1982	1967	1982	1967	1982
Employed								
Like very much	47.4	29.6	55.5	37.4	51.1	37.2	52.1	34.6
Like somewhat	36.7	46.4	27.7	42.3	30.8	42.8	31.6	42.2
Dislike	15.9	24.0	16.9	20.3	18.1	20.1	16.3	23.2
Total	100.0	100.0	100.0	100.0	100.0	100.0	100.0	100.0
N	268	492	336	437	360	337	964	1,266
Not employed								
Like very much	52.9	43.8	51.8	49.4	56.4	46.0	52.3	46.4
Like somewhat	32.2	44.9	37.2	39.3	33.4	41.7	35.0	41.0
Dislike	14.9	11.2	11.0	11.3	9.9	12.3	12.7	12.6
Total	100.0	100.0	100.0	100.0	100.0	100.0	100.0	100.0
N	481	316	422	373	405	467	1,308	1,156

[a] Age in 1982.

employed women and full-time housewives was greatest in this age group as well.

Reasons for such changes must be speculative at present. It is possible that women of this generation felt socially constrained to express satisfaction with the housewive role in 1967, but by 1982, with the changing climate of opinion, often among their own daughters, they felt free to express their opinions. Another possibility is that in 1967, housework may have been seen as a necessary part of child rearing, a valued role. By 1982 housework may have been defined as ordinary household tasks and thus less interesting and fulfilling. In any event, it does appear that by 1982, being employed outside the home was associated with lower satisfaction with housework. The relationship between housework satisfaction and employment may be due to a higher probability of entering the labor force among those women who were less enthusiastic about housework in 1967, as previous research suggests (Shaw 1983). It may also be the case that women who become strongly attached to their jobs change their views on housework, which may come to seem less interesting than outside employment. Further research in this area might bring new insights into the changes that have occurred in women's employment.

Appendix 1A

Table 1A–1
Regression Equations Predicting Attrition from the Original Sample

1967 Characteristics	Total Sample		Black		White[a]	
Highest grade completed						
Less than 12 years	.035	(2.4)	−.127	(4.4)	.058	(3.4)
Greater than 12 years	−.035	(2.0)	.045	(1.0)	−.037	(1.9)
Married, with children						
under age 18	−.061	(3.1)	−.036	(1.3)	−.068	(2.9)
Married, no children	.022	(0.8)	−.032	(0.8)	.021	(0.7)
In labor force	.026	(2.0)	.019	(0.7)	.025	(1.6)
Residence						
South	−.021	(1.5)	−.160	(5.6)	−.000	(0.0)
SMSA, central city	.073	(4.2)	.045	(1.4)	.062	(3.1)
SMSA, other	.061	(3.8)	.028	(0.7)	.062	(3.4)
Income, not reported	.078	(4.4)	.064	(1.9)	.074	(3.6)
Income above median	−.016	(1.0)	.012	(0.3)	−.021	(1.2)
Black	−.012	(0.5)	—		—	
Constant	.245	(10.1)	.416	(8.5)	.244	(8.4)
$\bar{R}^2$	.020		.072		.022	
N	4,845		1,291		3,554	

Notes: Excludes attrition due to death; these cases are not included in the regressions.

The absolute value of *t*-statistics is in parentheses.

[a]Includes 51 women of other races.

Notes

1. A more detailed description of the sampling procedure may be found in Center for Human Resource Research (1983).

2. The factors used to readjust the weights were years of school completed in 1967 and number of years in 1967 place of residence. See Center for Human Resource Research (1983) for further information.

3. CPS figures were calculated from U.S. Bureau of the Census (1985, table 13).

4. The NLS did not ask a question on highest grade completed in 1982. This question was asked in 1967 and 1977. In 1981 questions were asked on the date the respondent had completed high school or obtained a GED; at each interview after 1977, questions were asked on additional education obtained since the previous interview. The figures on high school completion in chapter 4 were obtained from a combination of these sources of information. It should be noted that figures from the CPS are not always based on self-reported information; reporting by other household members may affect the reliability of the data.

5. See Rhoton (1984).

References

Center for Human Resource Research. 1983. *The National Longitudinal Surveys Handbook*. Revised. Columbus: Center for Human Resource Research, The Ohio State University.

Rhoton, P. 1984. *Attrition and the National Longitudinal Surveys of Labor Market Experience: Avoidance, Control, and Correction*. Columbus: Center for Human Resource Research, The Ohio State University.

Shaw, L.B. 1983. "Problems of Labor Market Reentry." In L.B. Shaw, ed., *Unplanned Careers: The Working Lives of Middle-Aged Women*. Lexington, Mass.: Lexington Books.

Shaw, L.B., and O'Brien, T. 1983. "Introduction and Overview." In L.B. Shaw, ed. *Unplanned Careers: The Working Lives of Middle-Aged Women*. Lexington, Mass.: Lexington Books.

U.S. Department of Labor. Bureau of the Census. 1985. Current Population Reports. Series P-60, No. 147. *Characteristics of the Population below the Poverty Level, 1983*. Washington, D.C.: U.S. Government Printing Office.

2

The Employment Consequences of Different Fertility Behaviors

Frank L. Mott
Lois B. Shaw

T he mature women's cohort comprises women who were born between 1922 and 1936 and who were reaching adulthood between the late depression years and the mid-Eisenhower period. Thus these women began their work experience in a variety of economic, political, and social milieus. The oldest attained maturity during the end of the Great Depression, a period when jobs for women generally were not available and, in addition, work by women was frequently discouraged because it was thought to limit employment opportunities for men. The first half of the 1940s witnessed sharp increases in female employment, reflecting the employment demands of World War II. Although many women worked during that period, employment by women with young children was still atypical, and it is not clear to what extent fundamental societal values about women's work were genuinely altered. Nonetheless it is apparent that many women gained a taste for work during that period, inclinations with perhaps profound effects not only for those women but also for their children's generation.

The period following World War II witnessed the withdrawal of many women from the work force and an apparent return to the more traditional value systems of the prewar period. From a behavioral perspective, the roles and activities of young mothers in the late 1940s and 1950s, which represented the peak of the baby boom, may be described as stereotypical. A working mother with young children was atypical. In the 1960s, a period when many of the youngest women in this cohort began childbearing, the corner had been turned; women with young children began to seek employment in increasing numbers, although their work propensities were well below those of their counterparts who attained maturity in the 1970s. As a summary indicator, it is useful to note that the labor force participation rate for married women who had children under the age of 6 was only about 12 percent in 1950; in 1960 it was 18.6 percent; by 1970 it had climbed to 30.3 percent; and in 1985 it reached 50 percent. Thus in approximately a

We thank Mary Gagen for her expert assistance in completing the research for this chapter.

thirty-year period, the ability and/or inclination of a woman with preschool-age children to work has shifted from being a rare event to one that might almost be described as typical and certainly can be described as normatively acceptable.

This trend overlaps the attaining of adulthood of this cohort of women, as well as the NLS young women's cohort. The NLS cohort, most of whom were born between 1944 and 1954, became adults between the mid-1960s and mid-1970s. Their pattern of work activity and the extent to which employment during their early adult years may have affected their likelihood of maintaining subsequent employment ties has been analyzed previously (Shapiro and Mott 1979; Mott and Shapiro 1983). Those studies documented the considerable attachment to the work force of young women having their first child in the late 1960s and early 1970s and, in addition, suggested strongly that employment in the period immediately preceding and following a first birth was independently associated with employment several years later. This independent association was hypothesized to reflect stronger commitment to lifelong employment by those women who were known to have worked at a life-cycle point where women traditionally did not work (indeed, in 1970, only 24 percent of women with children under the age of 1 were in the labor force).

The Research

Within the context of this discussion, our research has several interrelated objectives. We will move backward in time to examine, to the extent the data permit, the employment trends of women who reached adulthood during the 1940s and 1950s and then consider the extent to which their early adult employment proclivities may have translated into later (contemporary) employment behavior. The employment measure utilized is the cumulative percentage ever employed after the woman's first birth, the only measure available. This measure is constructed from our knowledge of the date a woman indicates she first returned to work after her first child's birth. Its obvious limitation is that it will overstate actual employment at any specific post–first birth point because we have no knowledge about which women subsequently left employment and when they left. It is known that this older cohort showed a lesser attachment to the work force than more contemporary cohorts.

We first briefly describe the patterning of this employment in the decade following the birth of the first child for the women in this cohort who had children and show how this pattern varied by race and by educational attainment. Black women have historically had higher levels of labor force participation than white women, but less is known about racial differences in participation in the years immediately following child raising. It is also of some interest to note whether educational differentials in participation during this life-cycle stage are similar to those reported for more recent cohorts. Evidence from the younger women's cohort, as well as from other data sources, indicates that better-educated women have much higher levels of participation immediately before and after a first birth.

From a multivariate perspective, the focus in this research is on examining the extent to which work in the period immediately before and after a first birth (proxying here for early work commitment) is an important independent predictor of later employment. We will consider separately the determinants of contemporary employment for all mothers in the sample, as well as for women who had their first child in the 1950s. This latter birth cohort is of historical interest in its own right because it is representative of the baby boom cohort of American mothers. A particular focus will be on contrasting the association between earlier and later employment between black and white women. It is hypothesized that this linkage should be stronger for white women, given the knowledge that their postbirth employment during the 1940s and 1950s was less normatively acceptable and therefore perhaps indicative of a stronger employment commitment. Contemporary employment is defined here as number of weeks worked in either the 1972, 1977, or 1982 survey year—the year encompassing when the respondent was in the 45–49 age range.

In the context of a life-cycle model based on the theory of the allocation of time (Becker 1965; Schultz 1975), the hypothesis that early work activity would be positively associated with subsequent work activity is not surprising. In addition, it seems plausible to suggest that a major mechanism through which such a link will manifest itself is intervening fertility behavior (Jones 1981, 1982; Cramer 1980; Waite 1980). That is, women with strong work commitment at the time of the first birth will probably have had fewer children in the outcome year on average than those whose commitment was weaker. This fertility difference, in turn, will account for at least part of the difference in work activity between the two groups at that time.

It is possible that a link between early and later work activity could simply reflect the influence of the same factors on employment at different points in the life cycle. For example, women who at the time of their first birth had received more education or whose earnings potentials were greater are likely to retain these characteristics, and the effect of these characteristics will continue throughout the life cycle. If the link is based on measurable factors that influence the chance of employment, such as education or earning potential (Mincer and Polachek 1974; Sandell and Shapiro 1980), explicit consideration of these factors should account for variations in current work activity (in the outcome year), and knowledge of earlier work activity should add no new information in attempting to explain current work activity

(Heckman 1978). If, however, the link is based on unmeasurable factors, such as a taste for market work or a strong motivation to work based on a desire for upward mobility, then knowledge of earlier employment behavior will contribute to the explanation of current work activity because it will serve as a proxy for these unmeasured characteristics (assuming that those unmeasured factors are stable over time).

Additional possibilities for a link between early and later work activity may come from a direct effect of the former on the latter. That is, the work experience and skills acquired during employment around the time of the first birth add to the individual's stock of human capital and increase the opportunity cost of subsequent nonemployment beyond the level it would have achieved in the absence of such employment. Alternatively employment experience around the first birth may result in changes in unmeasured factors such as motivation or taste for work.

It is clear that there is a wide variety of explanations for a positive correlation between employment around the first birth and subsequent work activity. At the same time, each of the alternatives considered suggests that women with a strong motivation to work at the time of the first birth will probably have fewer children than those whose motivation is weaker and thus to be more likely to be employed during later periods of their life cycle. For this reason, we will focus on this mediating effect of intervening fertility by examining current work activity, controlling for current factors that influence work activity, including fertility dimensions, and controlling for whether the respondent was employed just before and just after the first birth.

In research with the younger women's cohort, it was hypothesized that employment in the periods immediately preceding and following a first birth should have independent effects on employment in 1978—a period at least five years after the birth of the respondent's first child—controlling for both contemporary (in 1978) standard labor supply factors and intervening fertility events (Mott and Shapiro 1983). It was hypothesized that work in the period immediately following the birth (defined in that analysis as within six months) should be the most powerful predictor of subsequent work activity because it probably represented the greatest commitment to work by a woman (that is, it was the time when employment was most difficult for a woman to maintain). The results were consistent with this hypothesis. In this research, we hypothesized that (1) in general, postbirth employment should be an even stronger predictor of subsequent work activity, reflecting the knowledge that work at that life-cycle point for earlier cohorts represented an even more unusual event and thus would have been even more a proxy for strong work commitment than work at that life-cycle point for women in the more recent young women's cohort; (2) employment in the period immediately after the birth should be a better predictor than employment immediately before the birth, reflecting the fact that returning to work right after a birth in all the periods under consideration was a less normative activity; and (3) early employment among white women should be a better predictor of contemporary employment than early employment among their black counterparts. For all of these hypotheses, the early employment effects for the 1950s baby boom group of mothers will be separately considered because it was in this historical period that employment was most exceptional.

The Sample

We consider the determinants of contemporary employment (weeks worked in the 1972, 1977, or 1982 survey year in which the respondent was aged 45–49) as a function of contemporary standard labor supply inputs as well as work attachment in the marriage–first birth interval and in the immediate post–first birth period. Models for all the black and white mothers in the sample, as well as women who had their first birth during the 1950s, are considered.

White and black mothers in the group were born between 1922 and 1936; most had their first child between the late 1930s and early 1960s. They thus overlapped the end of the depression years, the war years, and the peak baby boom years. It is likely that the implications of early adult employment on subsequent work activity may vary depending on when a woman attained adulthood. In addition, women who had their first child in the 1930s or in most of the 1940s were relatively young, reflecting a variety of social, economic, and political considerations. These young mothers were, on the average, less educated, southern born, and, on the basis of their early childbearing behavior, large family oriented. All of this suggests that from a labor force perspective, their shorter- and longer-term patterns of attachment might be quite different from the more typical woman who had a first birth during that period.

In contrast, the women in the sample who had a child after 1959 disproportionately include late childbearers; the youngest respondent in 1960 was already 24 years old. They are, in a sense, women from the baby boom generation who delayed childbearing, a behavior pattern atypical of women from their generation, perhaps because they had above-average work commitment. This finding is consistent with the knowledge that these post-1960 mothers, on average, have gone on to have somewhat fewer children than the earlier mothers in the group.

From a social and demographic perspective, the group of greatest interest are those who had their first child during the 1950s. These women are in all respects representative of the baby boom generation of mothers—in terms of their personal characteristics, as well as marriage and childbearing patterns.

Table 2-1
Characteristics of White Mothers in Regression Sample, by Time Period of First Birth

	Total	Before 1945	1945–1949	1950–1959	After 1959
Weeks worked in outcome year	30.1	24.3	28.2	32.0	30.8
Highest grade completed	11.5	9.8	10.9	11.9	12.4
Income less respondent earnings	18,254	14,396	17,617	19,216	18,062
Percentage living in South	29.5	45.6	30.0	27.3	23.1
Mean months since last birth	206	218	211	209	164
Mean number of children	3.8	4.3	3.6	3.8	3.1
Percentage working between marriage and first birth	46.9	25.2	37.6	52.6	63.4
Percentage working in first year after first birth	23.6	20.4	19.7	24.7	31.7
Age in 1982	52.5	57.6	55.6	50.7	48.6
Percentage with					
1972 being outcome year	37.2	97.1	63.9	17.8	9.1
1977 being outcome year	31.4	2.9	34.8	37.0	19.4
1982 being outcome year	31.1	0.0	2.3	45.2	71.5
N	2,050	206	543	1,115	186

It is fair to generalize about the baby boom generation of mothers from this sample. For this reason, a section of the analysis in this chapter will focus on this group.

Table 2–1 presents selected social, economic, and demographic characteristics of the black and white mothers considered in this analysis. The average white mother in the sample completed slightly fewer than twelve years of school compared with about ten years for her black counterpart. Consistent with the knowledge that, for the most part, they were reaching adulthood during the pronatalist late 1940s, 1950s, and early 1960s, they had large families: an average of 3.8 children for the white and 4.5 children for the black respondents. Close to half of the white mothers indicated that they had been employed at some time in the period between their marriage and when their first child was born. This employment is consistent with the fact that work by women without children was normatively acceptable. In contrast, only 24 percent of the white mothers indicated that they had worked at some time during the first year after the child was born. Work at this life-cycle point was clearly atypical and in most instances reflected either a commitment to the labor force or a strong economic need to contribute to family income, although a necessary caveat is that female employment during this life-cycle stage was somewhat more acceptable during the World War II period.

The early employment pattern of black women was somewhat different. Their level of prebirth employment was somewhat below that of the white women. This is because, on the average, many of the black women had their first child at an earlier age and thus had a shorter early adult period in which to be employed. For women in the sample who had a first child before marriage, the prebirth interval is defined as the gap between school leaving and first birth.

Whereas white employment declined sharply between the prebirth and postbirth periods, the converse was true for black women. Reflecting greater economic need as well as fewer social inhibitions against employment, black women maintained their employment ties in the postbirth period. Within the context of this study, which considers the independent impact of early employment on later employment, this finding suggests possible major differences between the temporal linkages for white and black women. Early postbirth employment was clearly more atypical for white than black women. As such, the average employed white mother may have been demonstrating a stronger psychological commitment to the work force in comparison with the typical young black worker. If this is the case, it may be hypothesized that early employment by a white mother will be a stronger independent predictor of later (at ages 45–49) employment than will be early reported employment by a black mother.

Trends in Postbirth Employment

Figure 2–1 contrasts the difference between the white and black employment patterns for the overall group of mothers, as well as for the 1950–1959 mother groups. Consistent with other evidence, black mothers from that era were much more likely than their white counterparts to work at all life-cycle stages. By the end of the first year, over 40 percent of the new black mothers had returned to work, and over 55 percent returned by the end of the second year. In contrast, only slightly over 20 percent of the white mothers returned during the first year and 30 percent by the second year. The racial gap shows no narrowing after that point.

It should be reemphasized that these employment distributions overstate actual employment levels in any given postbirth year because they do not take into account employment exits—a not inconsequential factor given that most of these women had additional children. An illustration of the importance of this factor is that about one-third of the white women who returned to work in the first year after their first child was born had worked in fewer than half

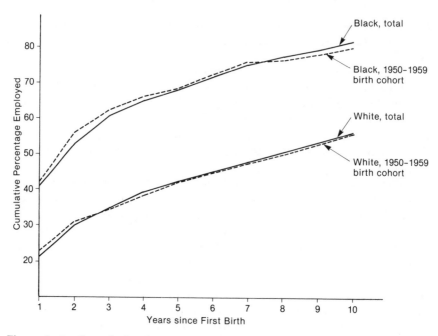

Figure 2–1. Cumulative Percentage Ever Employed after First Birth, by Race

the years between their first birth and 1982. In fact a few (about 7 percent) of these early returners had worked for six months or more in less than 10 percent of the years. At the other end of the scale, only about a quarter of these women had worked for six months or more for at least 90 percent of the time since childbearing began. Black women who returned in the first year were a little more likely to work fairly continuously; about one-third had worked in more than 90 percent of the years since their first return, but a substantial percentage of black women (27 percent) had also worked six months or more in fewer than half of those years.

Figure 2–2 suggests that this racial differential does not reflect large differences in educational attainment between the white and black women. Within racial groups, there are no major differences between the better and less educated in the propensity to return to work. This finding has several possible implications. First, it points to an overriding historical cultural difference in the propensity of black and white mothers to be employed. Second, the result is consistent with the notion that education was a less meaningful predictor of economic returns to employment for both black and white women in the past than is true now. Indeed many recent studies document substantial contemporary differences in employment between better- and less-educated women, regardless of race.

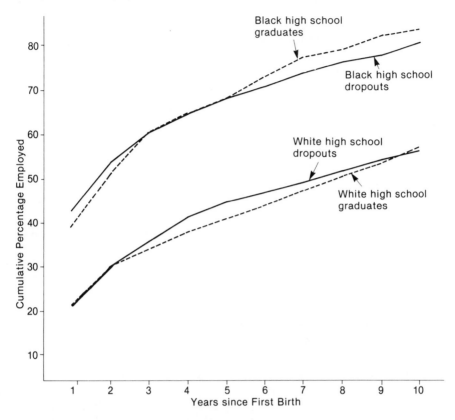

Figure 2–2. Cumulative Percentage Ever Employed after First Birth, by Race and Educational Attainment

Although we cannot pinpoint precisely the temporal placement of employment in the women's postbirth years, figures 2–1 and 2–2 suggest certain important racial differences. Table 2–2 focuses on one other dimension of the women's employment: the proportion of years between the first birth and a recent survey in which the women worked six months or more. Specifically we focus on the period between the woman's first birth and the personal interview (either 1972, 1977, or 1982), which encompassed the time period when the respondent was between the ages of 45 and 49. This table shows, consistent with figures 2–1 and 2–2, that black women, whether better or less educated, maintained much closer ties with the job market. There is some evidence, however, that better-educated women, particularly black women, had a stronger historic labor force attachment than their less-educated counterparts. This is certainly consistent with the notion that the ever-employed statistics in figures 2–1 and 2–2 mask the fact that the less-educated women were apparently more likely to have interrupted employment patterns.

Table 2–2
Mean Percentage of Years between First Birth and Survey Outcome Year in Which Repondent Worked Six Months or More, by Race and High School Completion Status

	Completed Fewer Than 12 Years' Schooling	Completed 12 Years or More of Schooling	Total
Total	36.3 (1,243)	38.6 (1,813)	37.8 (3,056)
White	33.1 (690)	37.2 (1,550)	36.0 (2,240)
Black	50.0 (553)	60.5 (263)	54.1 (816)

Note: Percentages are based on weighted data. Sample sizes are in parentheses. The survey outcome year is the personal interview survey year (1972, 1977, or 1982) that encompassed the period when the respondent was 45–49 years of age.

Conditioning Effects of Early Employment and Fertility Behavior on the Labor Supply Behavior of 45- to 49-Year-Old Women

In this final analytical section, we use ordinary least squares (OLS) techniques to examine the determinants of labor supply for women 45–49 years old as a function of standard labor supply explanatory variables, within a reduced form framework, augmented by two fertility variables (number of children the respondent has had and number of months since the birth of her last child) and three variables measuring work attachment immediately preceding and following the woman's first birth. These models generally parallel those used in analyses of the young woman's employment attachment (Mott and Shapiro 1983), with two important differences; the time span between first birth and the current employment outcome is much longer, and the variables measuring employment before and after the first birth are somewhat different. In the earlier analysis, the prebirth employment variable referred to a six-month interval preceding the first birth. Because of data constraints in this study, we are obliged to use the variable indicating whether the respondent was employed between marriage and first birth. Also in the earlier analysis, we focused on employment in the six-month period following the first birth. Given that it has been a long time since the first birth for the mature women in this study and the potential for recall error, we decided to focus here on employment during the first year after the first birth. We also added an additional postbirth variable: being employed for the first time in the second year after the first birth.

In this multivariate analysis, we estimate contemporary labor supply for all white and black mothers in the sample, as well as separately for women who had their first birth between 1950 and 1959. All of the models incorporate standard explanatory variables traditionally included in cross-sectional female labor supply models. That is, we include variables that proxy for factors considered to reflect female demand and supply of labor considerations, including education, other family earnings, labor market factors (size of labor force and area of residence), and fertility dimensions (age of youngest child and number of children). Additional period effects are controlled for by including the respondent's age, which effectively defines whether the outcome year was 1972, 1977, or 1982. In addition, the overall models include dummy variables specifying the time period when the respondent had her first birth (in relation to the omitted 1950–1959 reference period). Finally, and most important, all of the models include variables specifying whether the respondent worked in the marriage to first birth interval (school to first birth for those never married when they had their first child), or returned to work in the first year after her child's birth, and first returned to work in the second year following the birth.

The outcome variable in these models is weeks employed in the outcome year. The outcome year is the year preceding the 1972, 1977, or 1982 survey, selected on the basis of which year encompassed the point where the respondent was 45–49 years old. The full models are shown in table 2–3. The coefficients in the overall white model generally provide results consistent with expectations. Education was positive and highly significant, and other family income (primarily spouse's earnings) was negative and significant. The age of the respondent's last child was positively associated with current employment, but the number of additional children the woman had was not significant. This finding is consistent with many other studies that highlight the importance of children's ages but the lesser incremental importance of additional children. It is of some interest to note that neither the outcome year variable (proxied for by the respondent's age) nor the base fertility year variables were significant. Thus after taking the other factors into account, the historic period in which the woman had her first child does not seem to affect employment significantly in the outcome year. Finally, and of greatest interest from the perspective of this study, even with the standard explanatory variables in the model, consistent with expectations, employment in the periods immediately preceding and following the first birth are highly significant predictors of employment at ages 45–49.

The results suggested by the labor supply model for the black mothers differed from the white results in several important respects, including one of particular interest from the theoretical perspective of this study: employment after the first birth was not a significant predictor of subsequent work activity. This finding is consistent with our hypothesis that the more universal

Table 2–3

Estimating Weeks Worked in Outcome Year for All White and Black Mothers and for White and Black Mothers Whose First Birth Was between 1950 and 1959: Ordinary-Least-Square Regression Results

	All White Mothers	1950–1959 White First Birth Cohort	All Black Mothers	1950–1959 Black First Birth Cohort
Highest grade completed	1.93*	2.34*	1.71*	1.79*
Income less respondent's earnings	−.249*	−.245*	.023	−.120
Labor force size	−.933	−.235	−1.49	−1.010
South[a]	.215	.874	4.11***	1.43
Months since last birth	.043*	.049*	.015	.036
Number of additional children	−.211	−.117	−1.08*	−1.11***
Worked between marriage and first birth[a]	3.51*	3.63**	4.41**	2.49
Worked within year after first birth[a]	6.05*	2.74***	1.15	−1.57
First worked in second year after first birth	2.80	1.84	4.59	1.50
Age in 1982	−.106	−.216	−.744**	−.582
First birth before 1945[a]	−3.47	—	4.25	—
First birth 1945–1949[a]	−1.55	—	2.59	—
First birth 1960 or later[a]	−1.86	—	−2.75	—
Intercept	7.91	7.10	48.82*	40.31
R^2 (adjusted)	.114*	.109*	.107*	.095*
F	20.87	14.58	7.67	4.28
Sample size	2,050	1,115	728	313

[a]Specified category is coded 1. All others are coded 0. All variables not followed by [a] are continuous variables, as specified.

*Significant at .01 level.

**Significant at .05 level.

***Significant at .10 level.

historical acceptance of postbirth employment among black women implied a lesser unique commitment to employment among young black mothers relative to their white counterparts. Thus earlier employment would be less of an independent predictor of subsequent employment for black than for white respondents.

Focusing briefly on the models for women who had their first birth during the 1950s, essentially similar but perhaps slightly less satisfactory results may be noted. For the white mothers, the postbirth employment variable was somewhat less significant, and for the black mothers, the prebirth employment variable lost much of its statistical power. Thus our hypothesis that postbirth employment during the 1950s, given its non-normative implications, particularly for white women, would show the strongest association with contemporary employment, was not supported.

Conclusion

The historic patterns of employment for young American mothers in the 1940s and 1950s demonstrated the independent linkages between this early pattern of employment and more recent work attachment. It appears that white women with small children who worked during this earlier period were indeed showing unusual commitment to the workplace. These women were maintaining employment ties during a life-cycle stage when there were considerable social pressures to concentrate on home-related activities. The evidence we present, showing that white women who worked at that time are more likely to work now, independent of other contemporary social and economic forces, is consistent with this premise.

Also consistent with our hypothesis, the link between historic and contemporary employment for black mothers is much more tenuous. This finding may reflect the fact that black women were historically much more likely to be employed when they had small children than were white women. Undoubtedly closely linked with the fact that employment among black women was much more of an economic necessity, employment at that life-cycle point was culturally more acceptable for black mothers.

References

Becker, Gary, S. 1965. "A Theory of the Allocation of Time." *Economic Journal* 75: 493–517.

Cramer, James C. 1980. "Fertility and Female Employment." *American Sociological Review* 45:167–190.

Heckman, J.J. 1978. "Sample Statistical Models for Discrete Panel Data Developed and Applied to Test the Hypothesis of True State Dependence against the Hypothesis of Spurious State Dependence." *Annales de l'Inse* 30–31:227–269.

Jones, Elise F. 1981. "The Impact of Women's Employment on Marital Fertility in the U.S., 1970–75." *Population Studies* 35:161–173.

Jones, Elise F. 1982. "Ways in Which Childbearing Affects Women's Employment: Evidence from the U.S. 1975 National Fertility Survey." *Population Studies* 36: 5–14.

Mincer, J., and S. Polachek. 1974. "Family Investments in Human Capital: Earnings of Women." *Journal of Political Economy* 82:S76–S108.

Mott, Frank L., and Shapiro, D. 1983. "Complementarity of Work and Fertility among Young American Mothers." *Population Studies* 37:239–252.

Sandell, S.H., and Shapiro, D. 1980. "Work Expectations, Human Capital Accumulation, and the Wages of Young Women." *Journal of Human Resources* 15: 335–353.

Schultz, T.W. 1975. *Economics of the Family: Marriage, Children and Human Capital.* Chicago: University of Chicago Press.

Shapiro, David, and Mott, F.L. 1979. "Labor Supply Behavior of Prospective and New Mothers." *Demography* 16:199–208.

Waite, Linda J. 1980. "Working Wives and the Family Life Cycle." *American Journal of Sociology* 86:272–294.

3
Authority in the Workplace: Differences among Mature Women

Ronald D'Amico

S tatus attainment researchers reported a decade ago the surprising finding that cross-sectional samples of working men and women had nearly identical mean occupational status scores, as well as roughly comparable processes of occupational attainment (Treiman and Terrell, 1975; McClendon 1976; Featherman and Hauser 1976). Subsequent research established that these overall mean similarities mask substantial differences in occupational distributions and in mean job tasks. The heavy concentration of women in lower-level white-collar jobs is by now well known and has been the subject of extensive recent discussion. Increasingly clear is that these jobs generally offer less opportunity for advancement, pay less, provide less skill development, and are only rarely associated with the exercise of authority over others. Since Roos (1981) and Halaby (1979) found that differences in occupational placement account for a large portion of the mean wage gap between the sexes, understanding the processes generating sex segregation in occupational tasks continues to warrant careful scrutiny.

Of the occupational tasks on which men and women differ, authority in the workplace is one of the most inequitably distributed. By authority, I mean formal control over the work tasks or promotion prospects of others. Recent CPS data show that working women are half as likely as men to be in the manager, official, or proprietor occupational category. In other occupational categories as well, women are considerably less likely to be in positions where they direct or supervise the work tasks of others (Halaby 1979). Wolf and Fligstein (1979b) show that even net of sex differences in educational attainment and self-employment status, women are still much less likely than men to exercise authority in the workplace. Finally, even when they attain supervisory positions, women tend to be concentrated in less commanding positions—for example, they are clerical supervisors rather than managers (Robinson and Kelley 1979)—and are rarely found in top management positions of large corporations (Kanter 1977). This chapter lends further documentation to the distribution of authority among women and also models the determinants of work authority.

The importance of understanding the distribution of work authority derives from the far-ranging social, economic, and psychic consequences of an individual's possession of organizational power. For men authority has been shown to be strongly related to status and earnings (Robinson and Kelley 1979; Wright and Perrone 1977; Spaeth 1976). For women the returns to workplace power are more modest (Roos 1981), but sex differences in the propensity for men and women with equivalent characteristics to hold positions of authority account for a substantial part of the male-female gap in earnings (Halaby 1979; Roos 1981). Moreover, authority in the workplace has been shown to be related to values and political attitudes and behaviors (Dahrendorf 1959) and thus underlies important dimensions of stratification outside the workplace.

Reasons for Sex Differences in Workplace Authority

Why are women less likely than men to attain positions of authority? The literature suggests two broad categories of explanation. The first attributes the difference to the behaviors, attitudes, values, or abilities of women; the second explanation emphasizes the behavior of employers or the structure of opportunities in organizations.

Individual Explanations

Long-standing beliefs about innate or learned personality attributes of females hold that women are undesirous of assuming or incapable of carrying out leadership roles. Handicaps include passivity, lack of ambition, inability to give orders, and an overriding emotive attachment to the family. Such traits are held to derive from the socialization practices of families, schools, and the media, or, in the most biologically reductionist explanations, from natural predispositions (Kanter 1976). From whatever source, these feminine attributes make women poor management candidates.

A second variant of the individualist explanation assigns a greater role to cognitive processes but nonetheless arrives at similar conclusions. In the most well-developed variant of the argument, families are assumed to be rational economic units that allocate the labor of family members to market work and home work according to a schedule that maximizes overall family well-being (Becker 1965; Gronau 1973). As a result of such a calculus, women devote substantial portions of their adult lives to childbearing and child-rearing activities. Anticipating this, women enter occupations in the paid labor force that allow ease of exit and reentry access and do not require the learning of job skills that may erode during periodic interruptions of employment (Polachek 1981; Mincer and Polachek 1974). Consequently women have neither the background and training nor previous employment experience that would qualify them for management or other positions of authority.

Structural Explanations

Structural explanations argue that women are excluded from positions of authority by a structure of opportunity that is stacked against them. Statistical discrimination is one such mechanism by which women may be handicapped. In making hiring decisions, employers, who cannot be certain of the intentions or qualifications of individual applicants, rely on group-derived probabilities of job performance and quit rates (Thurow 1975). Aware of the tendency for women as a group to have irregular labor force participation patterns, employers may give men priority in hiring for any job for which a long-term labor force commitment is critical, including most management or other supervisory positions. Taken a step further, the statistical discrimination argument is used in dual labor market models to suggest that in general women are restricted to jobs offering low pay, poor opportunities for advancement, and unstable employment (Doeringer and Piore 1976). Other segmentation models, which also suggest women are systematically excluded from the more desirable employment opportunities, implicate more invidious and exploitative motives of employers (Edwards 1975).

One of the most compelling explanations for the systematic exclusion of women from managerial and other lucrative job slots is Kanter's (1977) model of organizational imperatives. Based on careful scrutiny of the inner sanctums of a large corporation, her insights suggest that the bureaucratic organization of corporate America gives rise to adaptive behavioral strategies of employees that are often mistakenly attributed to preexisting attitudes or dispositions of individuals. Thus managers, secretaries, and others act in predictable ways because workers in similar job slots are confronted with comparable organizational incentives, expectations, and uncertainties; individuals play the roles to which they have been assigned. This paradigm is useful in explaining both the exclusion of women from supervisory positions and the apparent weak labor force attachment of clerical workers, most of whom are female. On the first score, Kanter observes that managers are confronted with uncertainty and the need for exercising discretion in bureaucratic organizations that place a premium on predictability and routinized procedures. To reduce uncertainty in dealing with others, managers must rely on trust, mutual understanding, and shared values. These outcomes are fostered by considering for promotion to managerial ranks those with homogeneity in social background and organizational experience. By both criteria, women tend to be excluded.

Discounting the organizational experience of women, who tend to enter the bureaucracy largely in clerical positions, has additional consequences.

Well-qualified and capable women find themselves in positions with limited or nonexistent promotion ladders. This dead-end atmosphere prevails even though Kanter finds that many secretaries over time informally come to take over many of their bosses' discretionary functions and are therefore well prepared for more formally assuming managerial duties. But faced with dim prospects for advancement, these women come to exhibit characteristic irregular employment histories. The model that sees women's sporadic employment as causing occupational segregation is thereby stood on its head. In attempting to resolve this chicken-or-egg dilemma, Gronau (1982) finds support for the Kanter model by showing that wages at time 1 affect subsequent work plans and work history but that work plans at time 1 have no effect on subsequent wages.

Distribution of Authority among NLS Women

Although there are a number of models that attempt to account for the virtual exclusion of women from positions of authority and occupational sex segregation and male-female wage differentials more generally, I make no attempt to judge them. My aim, more modestly, is to describe the distribution of authority among the NLS women and to characterize the employment histories and other attributes of women possessing authority. Such an exercise will shed light on who exercises authority and where and how such authority is attained.

The occupational distribution of working women provides a first look at the extent to which women attain managerial rank (table 3–1). Results show that about 7.6 percent of NLS women working in 1982 were managers or administrators, all of whom can be assumed to exercise authority in the workplace. Figures from the CPS for comparably aged women are shown for the years 1972 and 1981 so change over the ensuing decade can be examined. Because this was a period of marked sensitivity to inequalities in work rewards, we might expect a consequent improvement in the status of women. The CPS figures show that the number of women who were managers increased from 6.5 percent of employed women in 1972 to 9.4 percent in 1981. Comparable CPS figures for men provide a point of reference. Men too increased their representation in the manager and administrative category by a nearly identical amount, though this change represents a proportionately greater increase for women than men. Together these figures show that both older men and women decreased their proportional representation in blue-collar jobs, that professional and managerial opportunities expanded for both sexes but at a faster rate for women, but that in 1982 men were still more than twice as likely as women to be in managerial positions.

While most managers can reasonably be assumed to exercise authority in

Table 3–1

Occupational Distribution of NLS and CPS Working Men and Women
(percentage)

	NLS, 1982[a]	CPS, 1972[b]	CPS, 1981[b]
Women			
Professional and technical	17.1	12.8	16.1
Managers and administrators	7.6	6.5	9.4
Sales	4.9	7.6	6.8
Clerical	35.5	32.1	32.5
Craft and kindred	1.9	1.6	1.9
Operatives	12.3	15.6	12.6
Nonfarm laborers	.4	.8	.9
Service	19.7	21.0	18.4
Farm workers	.7	2.0	1.4
N	1,735	6,318[c]	6,777[c]
Men			
Professional and technical		13.0	16.7
Managers and administrators		17.0	19.8
Sales		6.1	5.9
Clerical		6.7	5.8
Craft and kindred		23.4	22.0
Operatives		17.2	14.8
Nonfarm laborers		5.4	4.7
Service		6.7	6.7
Farm workers		4.6	3.6
N		10,139[c]	9,478[c]

Source: CPS figures are from U.S. Department of Labor (1982, pp. 635–649).

Notes: Figures are percentage distributions. The occupational coding scheme used for the NLS women is not exactly comparable to the one used in the CPS. Some differences between NLS and CPS figures are attributable to these coding differences.

[a]NLS women, ages 45–59, working in 1982.

[b]Employed persons ages 45–54.

[c]In thousands.

the workplace, not all those with authority are managers. Three questions from the 1982 women's survey can help uncover other positions of authority. The first asks, "Do you supervise the work of other employees, or tell them what to do?" followed by "About how many people do you supervise?" and then, "Do you have a say about their pay or promotion?" Table 3–2 shows a frequency distribution for each of these variables. Just under 30 percent of non-self-employed, currently working women report they supervise the work of others, but overwhelmingly most of them direct the work tasks of fewer than ten people. Only 6.4 percent supervise more than ten people, and, in

Table 3–2
Percentage of NLS Women Who Supervise Others

Question	Percentage
Do you supervise the work of other employees, or tell them what to do?	29.3[a]
About how many people do you supervise?[b]	
0	70.7
1–9	22.9
10 or more	6.4
Do you have a say about their pay or promotion?[c]	9.4[a]

Notes: Restricted to non-self-employed, currently working respondents.
[a]Percentage answering "yes."
[b]Not asked of those who answered "no" to the first question, for whom "0" was imputed.
[c]Not asked of those who answered "no" to the first question, for whom "no" was imputed.

results not shown in the table, only 1.6 percent supervise more than thirty workers. The final results from table 3–2 show that only about 9 percent of the NLS sample of working women report they have a say over the pay or promotion of others.[1]

Having responses to these questions for comparably aged men would provide a context within which to interpret these results. Unfortunately this same series of questions was not asked of the NLS men's cohort. However, Hill (1980) reports the responses to similar questions, asked of men aged 18–64, in the Michigan Panel Survey of Income Dynamics in 1976. Forty-six percent of non-self-employed working men reported they supervised other employees, and 26 percent reported they had a say over pay or promotion.[2] Thus women are substantially less likely than men to exercise either of these two dimensions of workplace authority.

Table 3–3 reports the distribution of authority by one-digit Census occupational codes. Those who supervise the work of others are concentrated in clerical, managerial, and professional occupations. The predominance in the clerical occupational category suggests that many women supervisors are actually in typical female occupations largely directing the work tasks of other women. Those with say over the pay or promotion of others are more concentrated in managerial occupations, but once again many are also found in the clerical category. Table 3–4 digs a bit deeper and reports the five three-digit occupations in which women in authority are most commonly found. The same occupations are the top five for both the supervision and pay and authority lists. These occupations are managers and officials not elsewhere classified (n.e.c.), clerical and kindred n.e.c., secretaries, nurses, and book-keepers. In these five occupations are found nearly half of all women who supervise others and over 60 percent of those with say over pay and promo-

Table 3–3
Distribution of Authority, by Occupation of Employment
(percentage)

	Percentage Exercising Authority in:	
Occupation	*Supervision*	*Pay or Promotion*
Professional and technical	24.2	23.0
Manager and official	19.7	34.0
Sales	3.3	.8
Clerical	32.3	31.3
Craft	3.6	3.8
Operative	3.7	.8
Nonfarm laborer	.2	—
Service	12.6	5.3
Farm workers	.4	.8
N	507	163

Note: The sample is restricted to non-self-employed currently working women who supervise others or have a say over pay or promotion.

Table 3–4
Most Common Three-Digit Occupations for Women in Authority

Those Who Supervise	*Those with Say over Pay or Promotion*
Managers, officials, proprietors n.e.c. (14.4%)	Managers, officials, proprietors n.e.c. (27.5%)
Clerical and kindred, n.e.c. (10.0%)	Nurses (8.7%)
Secretaries (8.7%)	Clerical and kindred (8.7%)
Nurses (8.1%)	Secretaries (8.3%)
Bookkeepers (4.7%)	Bookkeepers (7.5%)

Note: The universe is restricted to non-self-employed currently working women who exercise authority over others. Numbers in parentheses are percentages of women who exercise authority of the type shown who are in the named occupation.

tion. These figures once again suggest that with the exception of those who are managers, women who attain authority commonly do so in predominantly female job hierarchies.

Attainment of Authority

The structuralist and individualistic models give several reasons why women are underrepresented in positions of authority in the workplace. While not endeavoring to decide between these models, this section will nonetheless profile characteristics of women who attain supervisory responsibilities and gauge the handicap to promotion probabilities posed by a sporadic work history and pressing family responsibilities.

It is much harder to find evidence for a structuralist interpretation to data limitations in the NLS, but several factors from the individualistic model will be highlighted: work history information, measured by an item in the 1982 NLS asking respondents the number of years in which they worked six months or more since age 18 (and coded in interval categories); work attitudes, a series of questions asked in 1972 probing women about their attitudes regarding the employment of wives (such as, "A woman's place is in the home" with items coded on a four-point scale and summed, with high scores indicating favorable attitudes about the employment of wives);[3] number of children aged 0–17; and a household responsibility index measuring the degree to which the respondent has primary responsibility for household chores and maintenance.[4] Additional variables considered include education, race, marital status, and months of tenure with their current (1982) employer.

Table 3–5 reports means on these variables for women with and without authority. Results show some differences between these groups of women, but few of them are dramatic. Women with authority do have somewhat higher mean education levels, are more likely to be white, have somewhat fewer children, have work attitudes somewhat more favorable toward wives' employment, are more likely to have help with household chores, and have spent slightly more time in the labor force. The most notable difference is that women with authority have on average two years of additional tenure with their current employer, though even those without authority have accrued substantial tenure (over nine years) by the 1982 survey. Those with authority over pay or promotion are more highly selected out on all these traits than are those who merely supervise others. But with the exception of the tenure variable, differences between those with and without authority are slight. It does not seem, therefore, that the prior work histories, work attitudes, or household responsibilities of women currently with workplace authority were particularly consequential in making them eligible for promotion to supervisory ranks.

Table 3–6 reports results of logit analyses that examine in a multivariate framework the relationship between these characteristics and the probability of attaining authority. The first columns treat as the dependent variable the respondent's report about whether she supervises others. Despite the fact that table 3–5 showed that mean characteristics do not greatly distinguish those with and without authority, the logit results show a number of significant effects. Those who supervise others have higher education, reflecting the need for either training or credentials in authority positions. The race variable shows that whites are more likely than blacks to be in supervisory

Table 3–5
Means of Characteristics of Women with and without Workplace Authority

Variable	Total Sample	Women Who			
		Supervise	Do Not Supervise	Has a Say	Has No Say
Highest grade completed	12.03	12.58	11.78	12.81	11.94
Race (1 = white, 0 = other)	.88	.91	.87	.92	.88
Marital status (1 = married, spouse present, 0 = other)	.68	.68	.68	.64	.68
Age	51.70	51.60	51.75	51.39	51.74
Number of children, 0–17 years old	.43	.36	.46	.37	.43
Tenure (in months)	117.24	136.65	108.64	157.44	112.83
Years worked 6 months or more since age 18[a]	4.76	5.02	4.65	5.44	4.69
Work attitudes (high = favorable, low = unfavorable; range: 6–30)	21.15	21.64	20.93	22.13	21.04
Household responsibility index (hi = others do chores, lo = R does chores; range: 8–24)	12.79	12.94	12.73	13.23	12.75
N	1,735	508	1,227	163	1,571

Note: Non-self-employed currently working women only.

[a]Coded into categories with 0 = none; 1 = 1–5 years; 2 = 6–10 years; 3 = 11–15 years; 4 = 16–20 years; 5 = 21–25 years; 6 = 26–30 years; 7 = 31–35 years; 8 = 36–40 years; 9 = 41–45 years.

positions even net of the other variables in the equation. Tenure and, marginally, years worked six months or more since age 18 are also related to the supervision measure. Women with more stable and intensive patterns of work involvement are thus more likely to be found in positions of authority. This is not to gainsay the possibility that the perception of greater opportunities for promotion induced some women to remain in the labor market or with the same employer. In short, these results do not resolve the chicken-or-egg dilemma. But if we cannot be certain of the motivation underlying the decision to remain in the labor force, this result nonetheless suggests a payoff to greater work involvement and commitment.

Marital status and number of children are not significantly related to the log odds of attaining authority, but the household responsibility index is significant. Women who report that others in their household share house-

Table 3–6
Logit Analysis of Relationship between Background Characteristics and Authority in the Workplace

Independent Variables	Supervision		Pay or Promotion	
	MLE	Standard Error	MLE	Standard Error
Highest grade completed	.052*	.011	.063*	.017
Race (1 = white, 0 = other)	.242*	.068	.305*	.113
Marital status (1 = married, 0 = other)	−.079	.062	−.156	.096
Age	−.019*	.007	−.042*	.012
Number of children, 0–17 years	−.069	.038	−.071	.063
Tenure (in months)	.001*	.000	.001*	.000
Years worked 6 months or more[a]	.032*	.016	.072*	.028
Work attitudes	.010	.007	.019	.012
Household responsibility	.022*	.009	.042*	.014
Constant	3.997*	.420	3.588*	.676
N	1,784		1,782	

Note: Non-self-employed currently working women only. See table 3–5 and the text for more detail on the coding of variables.
[a]In categories; see table 3–5.
*Indicates $p \le .05$.

keeping duties are more likely to attain authority. Coverman (1983) found that the time expenditures men and women make to child care and household chores are inversely related to their hourly wage, all else equal. The results suggest that a heavy burden of household duties similarly retards the ability of women to advance to positions of authority in the workplace.

All variables significant in the equation with supervision as the dependent variable are also significant in the pay or promotion equation. More highly educated white women with more stable work history patterns and less burdened by household responsibilities are more likely to have a say over the pay or promotion of others.

Conclusions

This descriptive look at the attainment of authority among NLS women provides a number of interesting insights. Women are considerably less likely than comparably aged men to be in managerial occupations, but a look at Census data over the decade 1972–1981 suggests that the sex differential may be narrowing, at least in proportional terms. Using items from the 1982 survey that ask women whether they supervise others or have a say over the pay or promotion of others, we find that about 30 percent of non-self-employed, currently working respondents claim supervisory responsibilities and that just over 9 percent have a say over pay or promotion. Compared with PSID data reported by Hill (1980), women are two-thirds as likely as men to supervise others but only about one-third as likely to have a say over pay or promotion. Women with authority are distributed primarily over professional, managerial, and clerical occupations; the three-digit occupational data show that many women with authority report their occupation as nurse, secretary, bookkeeper, or clerical n.e.c. Probably women in supervisory positions are often overseeing the tasks of other female employees in largely female occupations. The occupational sex segregation of the labor force apparently persists even for women in authority. Kanter's (1977) observation that there are few promotion paths from clerical to managerial ranks thus looms as an important observation.

Individualistic and structural models take different approaches to explaining occupational sex segregation and the generally lower wages of women. The former implicate the behaviors and attitudes of women themselves, while the latter blame an opportunity structure biased against women or outright discrimination by employers. The structural model suggests that the work-related attitudes and behaviors of women are themselves shaped by a realistic appraisal of the nature of labor market opportunities. Without attempting to decide between these models and with no data on attitude formation or the motivation for prior work behavior, this chapter finds that years of education, previous work history, and household responsibilities are related to the probability of a woman's attaining workplace authority. The incentive structure is such, then, that at least some women who exhibit stable work patterns can attain supervisory rank. But this finding by itself says little about whether women and men with comparable characteristics have equivalent chances of being promoted nor does it shed light on what accounts for the gross sex disparity in the proportion of workers who are managers or who claim to exercise authority. Evidence uncovered by others (Hill 1980; Wolf and Fligstein 1979a) suggests the process of attainment is notoriously inegalitarian and generally works to the disadvantage of women.

Notes

1. It was assumed when the 1982 questionnaire was designed that the supervision question and the pay or promotion question constituted a Guttman scale. Consequently only those who answered "yes" to the first question were asked the subsequent question. Whether in fact these questions constitute a Guttman scale is unclear, but the assumption seems plausible.

2. The PSID also assumes these questions constitute Guttman scales. Differences between PSID men and NLS women in percentage answering "yes" could be due to age or period effects. However, Hill (1980) also reports results for PSID women aged 18–64, and the percentage answering "yes" are within 2 percentage points of the NLS estimates for both questions.

3. The specific items are: "A woman's place is in the home, not the office or shop," "A wife who carries out her full family responsibilities doesn't have time for outside employment," "Working wives lose interest in their homes and families," "A working wife feels more useful than one who doesn't hold a job," "Modern conveniences permit a wife to work without neglecting her family," and "A job provides a wife with interesting outside contacts." Responses were reordered to conform to a Likert scale with high values indicating favorable attitudes. The highest score possible is 30.

4. This index, from the 1982 survey, asks each respondent whether she has sole responsibility or whether others have responsibility or whether responsibility is shared for eight household tasks (grocery shopping, child care, cooking, cleaning dishes, cleaning house, washing clothes, yard and home maintenance, and family paperwork). Responses for each item are coded 1, respondent has sole responsibility; 2, responsibility is shared; and 3, others have sole responsibility. Responses to each item are then summed (range: 8–24).

References

Becker, Gary. 1965. "A Theory of the Allocation of Time." *Economic Journal* 75: 493–517.

Coverman, Shelley. 1983. "Gender, Domestic Labor Time, and Wage Inequality." *American Sociological Review* 48:623–637.

Dahrendorf, Ralf. 1959. *Class and Class Conflict in Industrial Society.* Stanford, Calif.: Stanford University Press.

Doeringer, Peter, and Piore, Michael. 1976. *Internal Labor Markets and Manpower Analysis.* Lexington, Mass.: Lexington Books.

Edwards, Richard. 1975. "The Social Relations of Production in the Firm and Labor Market Structure." In Edwards, Richard C., Reich, Michael, and Gordon, David M. (eds.), *Labor Market Segmentation.* Lexington, Mass.: Lexington Books.

Featherman, David, and Hauser, Robert. 1976. "Sexual Inequality and Socioeconomic Achievement in the U.S., 1962–1973." *American Sociological Review* 41: 462–483.

Gronau, Reuben. 1973. "The Intrafamily Allocation of Time: The Value of the Housewife's Time." *American Economic Review* 63:634–651.

———. 1982. "Sex-Related Wage Differentials and Women's Interrupted Labor Careers—the Chicken or the Egg." NBER Working Paper 1002.

Halaby, Charles. 1979. "Job-specific Sex Differences in Organizational Reward Attainment: Wage Discrimination vs. Rank Segregation." *Social Forces* 58: 108–127.

Hill, Martha. 1980. "Authority at Work: How Men and Women Differ." In Duncan,

Greg J. and Morgan, James N. (eds), *Five Thousand American Families. Vol. 8.* Ann Arbor: University of Michigan Press.

Kanter, Rosabeth Moss. 1976. "The Policy Issues: Presentation VI." *Signs* 1:282–291.

———. 1977. *Men and Women of the Corporation.* New York: Basic Books.

McClendon, McKee. 1976. "The Occupational Status Attainment Process of Males and Females." *American Sociological Review* 41:52–64.

Mincer, Jacob, and Polachek, Solomon. 1974. "Family Investments in Human Capital: Earnings of Women." *Journal of Political Economy* 82 (supplement):S76–S108.

Polachek, Solomon. 1981. "Occupational Self-Selection: A Human Capital Approach to Sex Differences in Occupational Structure." *Review of Economics and Statistics* 58:60–69.

Robinson, Robert, and Kelley, Jonathan. 1979. "Class as Conceived by Marx and Dahrendorf: Effects on Income Inequality and Politics in the United States and Great Britain." *American Sociological Review* 44:38–58.

Roos, Patricia. 1981. "Sex Stratification in the Workplace: Male-Female Differences in Economic Returns to Occupation." *Social Science Research* 10:195–224.

Spaeth, Joe. 1976. "Characteristics of the Work Setting and the Job as Determinants of Income." In Sewell, William H., Hauser, Robert M., and Featherman, David L. eds., *Schooling and Achievement in American Society,* New York: Academic Press, pp. 161–176.

Thurow, Lester. 1975. *Generating Inequality.* New York: Basic Books.

Treiman, Donald, and Terrell, Kermit. 1975. "Sex and the Process of Status Attainment: A Comparison of Working Women and Men." *American Sociological Review* 40:174–200.

U.S. Department of Labor. 1982. *Labor Force Statistics Derived from the Current Population Survey: A Databook. Vol. 1.* Washington, D.C.: U.S. Government Printing Office.

Wolf, Wendy, and Fligstein, Neil. 1979a. "Sex and Authority in the Workplace: The Causes of Sexual Inequality." *American Sociological Review* 44:235–252.

———. 1979b. "Sexual Stratification: Differences in Power in the Work Setting." *Social Forces* 58:94–107.

Wright, Erik Olin, and Perrone, Luca. 1977. "Marxist Class Categories and Income Inequality." *American Sociological Review* 42:32–55.

4
Returning to School at Midlife: Mature Women with Educational Careers

William R. Morgan

C urrent characteristics of adult education as "continuing" and "life-long" raise the issue of the extent to which the emergent pattern of extended participation in formal education constitutes a third career, parallel to but increasingly autonomous from family and work careers. Between 2 and 12 percent of adult Americans are pursuing various types of formal education, usually simultaneously with their family and employment responsibilities (National Center for Education Statistics 1981; U.S. Census Bureau 1984). Although this educational activity is interrelated with family and work roles in either a causal or coordinative manner, the term *career* suggests that increasingly this activity has its own internal thrust and is its own end. Current participation is highly contingent on prior experiences and future educational goals.

Variations in the historically dominant family careers of women have consisted of greater or smaller degrees of involvement in a relatively fixed pattern of activities prescribed from birth to death. Only recently have significant numbers of American working women had the opportunity to engage in occupational careers and to make decisions about the extent of their involvement independently of these traditional prescriptions about family responsibilities. This chapter examines whether significant numbers of women are now pursuing educational careers as a third line of autonomous activity. A brief discussion of the current social forces conducive to increased levels of adult education is presented, followed by two sets of analyses in which variations in rates of participation are described and then explained with reference to a set of prior family, employment, and education variables. For the most part these analyses are restricted to adult educational activity in colleges and universities as opposed to other forms of postsecondary institutions or sec-

My gratitude to Kenneth Chi for his excellent assistance with the data analysis.

ondary-level settings. Most adult education occurs in colleges and universities, and most information available in the NLS surveys concerns these settings. Adult education is further restricted to that which occurred between 1967 and 1982, the years when the NLS cohort of women matured from ages 30–44 to 45–59. Information on educational activity over this period was compiled from data available in eight of the ten interview rounds held during these first fifteen years of the survey.

Rise of Adult Education

Until recently adult education has been regarded as something of an anomaly in American society. Doubts about the quality of the typical adult education program and the qualities of adults who would spend their time in such activity in large part reflect the fact that the completion of one's formal education has traditionally been a social criterion for defining the end of adolescence and the onset of adulthood. Adult participation in formal education was considered exceptional behavior, appropriate mainly for those experiencing a difficult transition or disruption in their life course. Major cases in point have been wartime military veterans and displaced or empty-nest homemakers (those whose spouses or children, respectively, have recently left the household). Adult education prepared both groups for assuming new roles in the civilian labor force. The value of the additional education lay not only in the possibilities for new knowledge and certification but also in the psychological bridging experience of performing the role of student. A more recent entry into this category of transitional adults are dislocated and burned-out civilian workers seeking new occupational careers.

The second main category of individuals for which adult education has been a relatively normal and expected occurrence are those for whom an updated knowledge base is vital to their job performance, especially those in the education and health professions. Their continuing education in many instances may be mandated by employers. The proximity of most professional workers to postsecondary institutions and their familiarity with the classroom makes formal adult education to them little different from the informal, on-the-job training experiences of most other workers.

The third category of traditional adult student is the individual working toward graduate-level certification on a part-time basis. These persons find it necessary to continue their course of study well past adolescence and into adulthood because of financial or other personal constraints that prevent their full-time student status. The increasing demand for graduate degree holders and the relatively high cost of this form of education have greatly expanded this segment of the traditional adult student population.

An even more widespread normalization of the adult student role may now be occurring. In large part this reflects the decreasing number of hours per day that the average adult must spend in combined work and household responsibilities. How to make meaningful use of one's free time, somewhat uneasily labeled leisure time (Robinson 1977), has become an increasing concern in the lives of contemporary American adults. One possible use of this new free time is to take a course at a nearby college. Many adults who elect to try this activity view it only as a recreational alternative, perhaps something one does during an off-night for television viewing. Other adults, however, perceive their course-taking activity as a normal extension of a serious, albeit gradual, educational career.

In addition to the time constraint, the barriers of tuition expense and physical access have also been reduced for this education-prone adult. Bishop and Van Dyk's (1977) study of 1970 adult education participation in eighty-eight metropolitan areas found that attendance rates varied directly with the lowered tuition costs and physical presence of a public two-year college in the area. Since their study, an even stronger institutional impetus has been created by the new availability of empty classrooms in many of these local colleges and universities. When the aging of the postwar baby boom birth cohorts diminished the traditional college-age student population, many college administrators began in the 1970s to look toward the adult market as a possible solution to budget deficits (Kline, Livesey, and Stern 1975). Vigorous media advertising and other forms of promotional activity have become commonplace in efforts to attract adults back to the classroom.

There is also some evidence that the traditional popular association of education with the age of adolescence may now be diminishing. Hogan (1978) and Marini (1983) have reported considerable variation among more recent birth cohorts in the sequencing of the major transitional life events of school completion, first full-time job, marriage, and children. Approximately one of every four adults in their samples completed their formal education after taking their first full-time job. This nontraditional sequence may signal a more general tendency toward the relaxation of age-graded behavior norms, particularly regarding the appropriate age for the student role. The increasing level of educational attainment among successive birth cohorts in the American population should strengthen this tendency, given the longer time requirements for higher levels of attainment.

The net result of these forces has been a dramatic shift over the past decade in the age composition of the college student population. The proportion of the total student population who are age 25 and over has climbed steadily from 27.9 percent in 1972 to 37.2 percent in 1983 (U.S. Bureau of the Census 1984). Among female college students, the proportion of adults has jumped from 25.8 percent to 39.6 percent.

Education over the Life Course

The main question in this first set of descriptive analyses is how the recent formal educational experiences of mature women relate to their educational attendance patterns over the life course. According to the 1982 survey, an estimated 900,000 of the 16.8 million women in this 1922–1936 birth cohort attended some college in the previous year. This number represents 5.4 percent of all American women ages 45–59. Both degree credit and noncredit courses are included in this total, and the reported length of attendance varied from one week to the full year. The modal length of attendance was ten to fourteen weeks, the approximate duration of a quarter- or semester-length course.

A broader definition of adult education also includes participation during the past year in formal training programs other than college courses or on-the-job training programs. Including these participants increases the total in adult education to 1.6 million women, or 9.4 percent of the cohort. The modal length of these training experiences was one to four weeks; they took place in a variety of settings, including high schools, vocational schools, community colleges, and four-year colleges. Such training is clearly an important component of the total picture of adult education, particularly that which is geared toward occupational career enhancement. Training participation, however, will not be further analyzed in this chapter. Adult education will be restricted to that involving college attendance for noncredit or degree credit coursework, including undergraduate and graduate-level activity. Participation in regular schooling at the secondary level will also be briefly examined, but it is not the focus of this chapter because so few women ages 45–59 take high school coursework (an estimated 0.4 percent in 1982). The exclusion of training activity will, of course, bias any assessment of the extent to which adult education is the extension of an educational career separate from one's occupational activity. At the same time, however, this restriction should facilitate a clearer specification of the causal parameters of college level adult educational activity.

Table 4–1 presents the incidence of college attending by mature women over the fifteen years from 1967 to 1982 and within each of the three five-year periods. These frequencies are also calculated separately for women grouped into three birth cohorts and black-white racial status. Overall 22.4 percent of the women attended college at least once during the fifteen-year period. The table reveals the expected higher attendance rates for whites in addition to substantial birth cohort and period differences. Attendance rates increase linearly and additively the more later born the cohort and the more recent the time period. The lowest five-year attendance rate, 8.1 percent, occurred during 1967–1972 for women in the 1922–1926 birth cohort, and

Table 4–1
Percentage of Mature American Women 45–59 in 1982 Who Attended Some College during 1967–1982, by Birth Cohort and Race

Intervals of College Attendance	Year Born			Race		
	1922–1926	*1927–1931*	*1932–1936*	*Black*	*White*	*Total*
1967–1972	8.1	9.0	10.7	6.2	9.6	9.2
1972–1977	8.6	12.9	13.4	8.5	11.9	11.6
1977–1982	10.6	17.0	19.5	10.0	16.3	15.6
1967–1982	16.8	23.4	27.5	14.4	23.5	22.4
N	1,239	1,142	1,161	959	2,583	3,542

Note: Percentages in this and later tables in this chapter are corrected using 1982 sampling weights.

the highest, 19.5 percent, was during 1977–1982 for women in the 1932–1936 cohort.[1]

The period differences represent confirming evidence for the secular increase in adult education participation previously documented only in Census time-series data. The birth and race cohort differences in adult college attendance are attributable mainly to lower levels of high school completion among earlier-born black women. Individuals without secondary-level certification usually cannot take college-level coursework, and high school completion rates differ substantially across the cohort groups. Table 4–2 indicates that one-third of all women born between 1922 and 1926 had not completed high school by 1982, compared to one-fifth of the women born between 1932 and 1936. Members of the 1922–1926 cohort carried the historical impediment of maturing to the usual age of high school completion during World War II, in addition to the parental background disadvantage accruing from the normal upgrading in the origin status of successive American birthrates. The racial difference in completion rates is even more marked: half the black women in the total cohort, compared to one-fifth of the whites, are noncompleters. Continued recent improvements in high school completion rates, particularly among ethnic minorities (Morgan 1984, p. 215), can thus be expected to expand further the pool of adults available to attend college.

Table 4–2 shows the amount of postsecondary level certification achieved by these women in 1982. Only 14 percent had any postsecondary degrees, including 3 percent with associate's degrees, 8 percent with bachelor's degrees, and 3 percent with various graduate degrees. The proportion with postsecondary certification again varied substantially across the birth and race cohorts, ranging from 9 percent for the 1922–1926 cohort to 17

Table 4–2

Percentage Distribution of Highest Level of Educational Certification Achieved by 1982, for Mature American Women 45–59, by Birth Cohort and Race

Highest Certification Level	Year Born			Race		
	1922–1926	1927–1931	1932–1936	Black	White	Total
None	32.1	25.1	21.5	51.3	23.6	26.4
High school diploma or GED	58.4	59.7	61.4	39.9	62.0	59.8
Associate degree	2.3	3.3	2.7	1.6	2.9	2.8
Bachelor degree	5.1	8.9	11.2	3.8	8.8	8.3
Graduate degree	2.0	3.0	3.2	3.4	2.6	2.7
N	1,203	1.114	1.132	912	2,537	3,449[a]

[a]Information on certification level unavailable for ninety-three women.

percent for the 1932–1936 cohort and 9 percent for black women compared with 14 percent for whites. Of interest here is what proportion of these women achieved their higher levels of certification as adults.

Table 4–3 indicates how many of the three five-year periods between 1967 and 1982 the women attended some college, with the women grouped according to their 1982 certification levels. The number of periods during which a woman attended is a rough index of her college attendance activity level over the fifteen-year period.[2] The strong relationship in this table between activity and certification levels is striking. Fully 90 percent of the graduate degree women attended college at least once during the fifteen-year span, and 26 percent attended during each of the three periods. For the women at other levels, the percentage who attended once increased linearly from under 2 percent for the high school noncompleters, 21 percent for the high school completers, 61 percent for associate's degree holders, and 69 percent for bachelor's degree holders.

Tables 4–4 and 4–5 present for women in each certification category the year and age when her certification was achieved. These distributions show more precisely the extent to which the different levels of adult education activity associated with each certification level did in fact generate that certification. These distributions also provide an indication of the great differences in the lengths of the educational careers of women in each certification level. Over half the graduate degree holders in 1982 (54 percent) received their degree during the preceding fifteen years. A total of 17 percent of the bachelor's degrees and 25 percent of the associate's degrees also came after 1967. By comparison, for the modal category of women who were terminal high

Table 4–3
Number of Five-Year Intervals between 1967–1982 of College Attendance, by Highest Level of Educational Certification Achieved

Number of Five-Year Intervals Attended	Highest Certification Level					
	None	High School	Associate	Bachelor	Graduate	Total
0	98.5	79.1	39.2	31.3	9.9	77.3
1	1.4	12.9	17.7	26.8	22.3	11.4
2	.1	6.8	33.6	26.8	41.7	8.4
3	0	1.1	9.5	15.1	26.1	2.9
N	1,123	1,898	84	254	90	3,449

Table 4–4
Cumulative Percentage Distribution of Year When Highest Level of Educational Certification Achieved, within Birth Cohorts and Certification Levels

Year Certified[a]	Year Born			
	1922–1926	1927–1931	1932–1936	Total
None				
Before 1938	30.8	5.6	2.6	15.1
1938–1942	82.1	31.2	8.1	49.1
1943–1947	98.4	91.1	22.2	75.1
1948–1952	99.4	99.1	86.6	95.8
1953–1957	99.5	99.3	98.6	99.2
1958–1962	99.5	99.4	99.2	99.4
1963–1967	99.9	99.5	99.2	99.6
1968–1972	100.0	99.9	99.6	99.9
1973–1977	100.0	100.0	100.0	100.0
1978–1982	100.0	100.0	100.0	100.0
N	384	316	279	979
High School				
Before 1938	2.2	0.2	0.0	0.8
1938–1942	59.1	2.0	1.0	21.0
1943–1947	93.4	60.9	1.4	52.2
1948–1952	93.8	95.4	54.7	81.4
1953–1957	94.5	96.1	94.7	95.1
1958–1962	95.9	96.6	96.0	96.2
1963–1967	97.0	97.2	96.9	97.2
1968–1972	98.5	98.2	97.7	98.2
1973–1977	99.6	99.5	99.1	99.4
1978–1982	100.0	100.0	100.0	100.0
N	643	606	649	1,898
Associate				
Before 1938	0.0	0.0	0.0	0.0
1938–1942	12.7	0.0	0.0	3.7

Table 4–4 continued

Year Certified[a]	Year Born			
	1922–1926	*1927–1931*	*1932–1936*	*Total*
Associate (*continued*)				
1943–1947	73.7	10.9	0.0	26.0
1948–1952	82.8	70.8	3.9	54.0
1953–1957	82.8	74.5	57.0	71.6
1958–1962	87.5	74.5	58.4	73.4
1963–1967	88.5	74.5	63.0	75.1
1968–1972	97.5	81.3	71.6	83.1
1973–1977	98.9	89.0	74.1	87.4
1978–1982	100.0	100.0	100.0	100.0
N	26	30	27	83
Bachelor				
Before 1938	0.0	0.0	0.0	0.0
1938–1942	2.0	0.0	0.0	0.4
1943–1947	50.6	3.3	0.0	11.9
1948–1952	78.4	54.5	0.6	36.2
1953–1957	80.8	74.9	52.5	66.4
1958–1962	82.9	81.7	75.6	79.3
1963–1967	84.9	83.0	81.4	82.7
1968–1972	87.4	92.7	87.6	89.4
1973–1977	95.0	96.7	91.7	94.2
1978–1982	100.0	100.0	100.0	100.0
N	57	84	113	254
Graduate				
Before 1938	0.0	0.0	0.0	0.0
1938–1942	0.0	0.0	0.0	0.0
1943–1947	5.3	0.0	0.0	1.3
1948–1952	13.0	7.6	0.0	6.0
1953–1957	32.0	22.7	1.0	19.6
1958–1962	39.3	28.2	27.3	30.5
1963–1967	59.0	40.4	43.4	46.1
1968–1972	87.6	57.3	61.2	66.2
1973–1977	100.0	81.2	86.3	87.8
1978–1982	100.0	100.0	100.0	100.0
N	23	32	34	89

[a]Year certified for the "none" category is year last attended regular schooling.

school completers, less than 3 percent attained their secondary certification during the fifteen-year period after 1967.

The actual age of certification shows most directly the extent to which these women's educational careers have extended well into adulthood. Those whose highest certification came at age 25 or later include 5 percent of terminal high school completers, 29 percent of the associate's degree holders, 27 percent of the bachelor's degree holders, and almost all (92 percent) of the graduate degree holders. Even more remarkable is the percentage of women

Table 4–5
Percentage Distribution of Age When Highest Level of Educational Certification Achieved, for Mature Women 45–59, in 1982

Age Certified[a]	None	High School	Associate Degree	Bachelor Degree	Graduate Degree
Total					
Under 15	49.1	4.1	1 2	0.0	0.0
15–19	48.6	89.0	29.6	6.3	1.3
20–24	1.2	1.8	39.9	66.3	6.9
25–29	0.2	0.6	1.3	6.2	18.5
30–34	0.0	0.8	1.4	4.4	10.3
35–39	0.1	1.4	4.7	4.6	25.9
40–44	0.3	1.2	6.6	3.8	12.8
45 and over	0.0	1.0	14.9	8.3	24.3
	100.0	100.0	100.0	100.0	100.0
N	1,123	1,898	84	254	90
Blacks					
Under 15	48.4	8.1	0.0	0.0	0.0
15–19	46.7	69.6	5.7	13.4	0.0
20–24	2.2	8.6	24.9	35.7	6.6
25–29	0.6	2.8	0.0	9.8	20.0
30–34	0.2	1.8	0.0	4.9	24.1
35–39	1.3	4.2	12.0	9.9	6.5
40–44	0.6	1.7	18.9	2.7	26.6
45 and over	0.0	3.2	38.5	23.6	16.2
	100.0	100.0	100.0	100.0	100.0
N	525	320	13	34	20
Whites					
Under 15	49.3	3.8	1.3	0.0	0.0
15–19	49.0	90.4	31.0	6.1	1.4
20–24	1.1	1.3	40.9	67.7	7.0
25–29	0.3	0.4	1.4	6.1	18.4
30–34	0.0	0.7	1.5	4.3	8.4
35–39	0.0	1.2	4.2	4.4	25.4
40–44	0.3	1.1	6.2	3.8	14.1
45 and over	0.0	1.1	13.5	7.6	25.3
	100.0	100.0	100.0	100.0	100.0
N	598	1,578	71	220	70

Highest Certification Level spans None, High School, Associate Degree, Bachelor Degree, Graduate Degree.

[a]Age certified is age last attended regular school for the "none" category.

whose certification came at age 45 or later: 1 percent of the terminal high school completers, 15 percent of the associate's degree holders, 8 percent of the bachelor's degree holders, and 24 percent of all graduate degree holders.

Furthermore, for black women the age of completion tended to be even higher across all certification levels except graduate degrees. The very small sample sizes for blacks in these higher certification categories, however, makes this last finding only suggestive. Given the previously reported figure that in 1982 5 percent of the cohort were still educationally active, one can expect that the overall level of certification in the cohort will continue to increase for at least another five years. Thus the percentage of women in the higher degree categories whose degrees came relatively late in their life course will shift even higher.

The nature of the adult education experience of these women is also suggested by the content of what they studied. Although these courses of study cannot be determined precisely, table 4–6 categorizes into nine groups the major field of college study reported in their 1981 or 1982 interviews for the 22 percent who attended some college during the 1967–1982 period. This distribution is broken out separately for the birth and race cohorts and by 1982 certification level.

Overall approximately 30 percent of the women reported an arts and sciences or general studies concentration and 50 percent a professional field (education, business, health, or home economics); 20 percent could give no particular major area of study. This distribution held fairly consistently across birth cohorts, but the fields of black women differed slightly from whites in two respects: black women studied less frequently in the arts and sciences — 12 percent compared to 21 percent — and more frequently in education — 30 percent compared to 19 percent.

Causes of Adult College Attendance

These last analyses focus on the extent to which the prior educational activity and future educational plans of these women determined their adult education participation net of five other major sets of determinants: their origin status and locational characteristics, prior labor market activity, household characteristics, and changes in household characteristics. A final analysis looks at the effect of the amount of adult education activity net of these other explanatory variables on subsequent employment behavior.

Figure 4–1 presents two heuristic causal diagrams of the hypothesized structural relationships. In model 1, influences on three dependent variables are estimated: college attendance prior to 1967, educational plans in 1967, and college attendance between 1967 and 1982. In model 2, factors influencing college attendance in each of the five year periods are examined.[3]

Table 4–6
Major Field of Study of 1968–1982 College Attenders, by Birth Cohort, Race, and 1982 Certification Level
(percentage)

Field of Study	Year Born			Race		Certification Level				Total
	1922–1926	1927–1931	1932–1936	Black	White	High School or Less	Associate's	Bachelor's	Graduate	
Arts and humanities	8.5	9.5	10.1	1.9	10.0	8.3	4.7	12.5	12.7	9.5
Social sciences	6.5	6.2	8.0	6.1	7.0	4.9	0.0	14.8	4.3	7.0
Math and science	4.2	3.6	3.1	4.3	3.5	4.0	0.0	4.5	1.5	3.6
Education	17.4	20.1	19.8	29.6	18.6	4.7	7.6	40.1	56.4	19.3
Business and commerce	19.9	14.7	14.7	11.9	16.3	21.3	30.6	6.9	0.0	16.0
Health professions	8.6	12.4	12.9	7.7	11.9	10.1	40.0	10.4	3.6	11.6
Home economics	3.7	5.0	1.8	.6	3.6	2.2	0.0	6.3	4.9	3.4
General and other	5.7	8.2	9.3	9.1	7.9	8.1	15.0	3.7	10.2	8.0
Unreported	25.4	20.3	20.3	28.8	21.1	35.8	2.1	0.7	6.3	21.6
	100.0	100.0	100.0	100.0	100.0	100.0	100.0	100.0	100.0	100.0
N	192	234	290	115	601	398	52	180	79	716

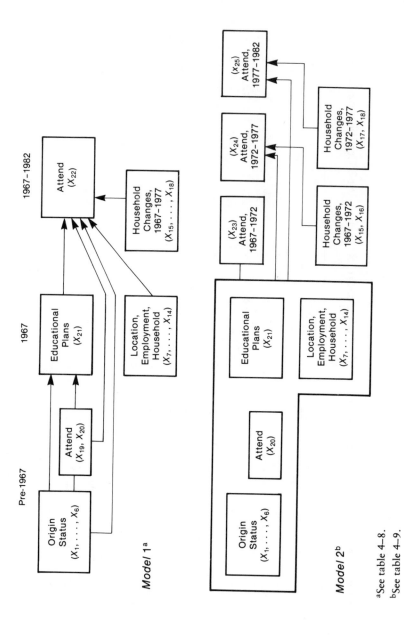

Figure 4–1. Two Heuristic Causal Models of Adult College Attendance

[a]See table 4–8.
[b]See table 4–9.

Table 4–7
Weighted Means and Standard Deviations for Variables in Equations for Adult College Attendance and Employment of Mature Women, 1982 Respondent Sample

Variable Name[a]		Mean	S.D.
Origin status			
X_1	Hd. educ., yrs.[b]	8.435	3.473
X_2	Hd. occ., Dun. SEI[c]	29.581	21.738
X_3	Mother employed	0.304	0.460
X_4	Black	0.102	0.303
X_5	Age, 1967	37.154	4.343
X_6	H.S. academic performance	4.398	2.168
Location, 1967			
X_7	Residence (non-SMSA)		
	City	0.310	0.462
	Suburb	0.410	0.492
X_8	South	0.310	0.462
X_9	Area unemployment rate	4.238	1.823
Labor market activity, early			
X_{10}	Employed, 1963–1967 (none)		
	Teaching	0.045	0.208
	Nursing	0.040	0.196
	Other professional or managerial	0.055	0.229
	Clerical, retail	0.254	0.435
	Operative, craftsperson	0.120	0.325
	Service, laborer	0.138	0.344
Household characteristics			
X_{11}	Health impaired, 1967	0.166	0.372
X_{12}	Hus. occ. 1967, Dun. SEI	40.64	23.52
X_{13}	Marital status 1967, single	0.145	0.352
X_{14}	Children, no. 1967	2.714	1.947
X_{15}	Marital status change 67–72 (no ch.)		
	New single	0.064	0.244
	New married	0.028	0.166
X_{16}	Children, no inc. 67–72	− 0.377	0.995
X_{17}	Marital status change 73–77 (no ch.)		
	New single	0.070	0.255
	New married	0.032	0.177
X_{18}	Children, no. inc. 72–77	− 0.712	1.031
Educational activity			
X_{19}	Educ., yrs. attain. 1967	11.261	2.758

Table 4–7 continued

Variable Name[a]	Mean	S.D.
X_{20} Attend coll., by 1967	0.180	0.384
X_{21} Educ. plans, 1967	0.327	0.469
X_{22} Attend coll., 67–82	0.224	0.417
X_{23} Attend coll., 67–72	0.092	0.289
X_{24} Attend coll., 72–77	0.116	0.320
X_{25} Attend coll., 77–82	0.156	0.363
X_{26} Attend coll., 67–82, no. of intervals	0.364	0.753
Labor market activity, recent		
X_{27} Employed, any occ., 77–82	0.735	0.441

Note: $N = 3,542$.

[a]Referent category for each multiple-dummy variable (X_7, X_{10}, X_{15}, X_{17}) is given in parentheses after variable name.

[b]Education in years of the Head of Household.

[c]Head of Household's Occupational Status in Duncan Socio-economic Index.

Variable Measurement

Table 4–7 gives the means and standard deviations of all variables entered in the equations. Six variables are used to measure the woman's origin status. Education in years (X_1) and occupational status (X_2) in Duncan Socio-economic Index (SEI) units were measured for the respondent's head of household when she was 15. Also included were whether her mother was employed when the respondent was 15 (X_3), whether her race was designated black (X_4), her age (X_5), and the self-report of her high school academic performance (X_6), a sum of responses to two questions on how well she did in English and math. Three characteristics of her location in 1967 were measured: a multiple dummy variable for whether she lived in the city or suburb of an SMSA (X_7), another dummy variable for residence in the South (X_8), and the CPS measure of the unemployment rate of her area (X_9). Early labor market activity (X_{10}), was measured by a six-term dummy variable coded 1 if the woman had a current or last occupation of two weeks or more in the past five years (1963–1967) in one of six categories: teaching, nursing, other professional or managerial, clerical or retail sales, operative or craftsmen, and service worker or laborer. The referent category was not employed.

The characteristics of the woman's household in 1967 were measured for four variables: whether she reported a health impairment that prevented her from working (X_{11}), the Duncan SEI score of her husband's occupation (X_{12}) (with race-specific mean values assigned for any woman without a husband), the number of children living in the woman's household (X_{13}), and whether her marital status (X_{14}) was single (comprising divorced, widowed, and separated). Four variables measured change in household characteristics. Two were the change in the number of children living in the household between 1967 and 1972 (X_{16}) and between 1973 and 1977 (X_{18}). The other two were two-term dummy variables for a change in marital status to either single or married, from 1967 to 1972 (X_{15}), and from 1973 to 1977 (X_{17}), with the referent category for each variable being no change.

Educational activity variables included the fifteen-year (X_{22}) and three five-year (X_{23}, X_{24}, X_{25}) period measures of adult college attendance and the number of periods attended (X_{25}). These were as defined in tables 4–1 and 4–3. Also measured was having plans for further education (X_{21}), coded to 1 for any positive response to the 1967 interview question, "Are you planning to enroll in any type of educational or training courses in the future?" Educational attainment level in 1967 was measured either by highest year completed in 1967 (X_{19}) or by whether the respondent attended any college by 1967 (X_{20}). The first, interval form, was used whenever this variable was entered as an explanatory variable; otherwise the second, binary form, was used.

Findings

The equation estimates reported in tables 4–8 and 4–9 provide strong support for the hypothesized relationships. The variable having the strongest direct effect (as indexed by the size of the probit coefficient relative to its standard error) on adult college attendance, whether measured over the full fifteen years or in each five-year period, was having educational plans in 1967. As would be expected, this variable had its strongest effect on attendance in the first five-year period. The second strongest direct effect on attendance came from 1967 educational attainment level, which also had a strong indirect effect by increasing the likelihood that a woman had further educational plans. The variable having the third strongest effect on attendance was high school academic performance level. In addition to its significant direct effect on adult college attendance, it had strong and significant indirect effects by raising both attainment levels and the likelihood of further plans.

Also apparent in these results is the strong underlying importance of a woman's origin status. This effect, however, operates only indirectly on eventual adult college attendance by the impact of a woman's parents' education and occupation on her early educational attainment.

Of the three remaining sets of variables in the equations, all have significant direct effects on attendance, as well as indirect effects by plans. The measure of early labor market activity shows somewhat stronger effects, though, than the household and locational characteristics. Having been employed in any occupation except the blue-collar and other professional categories increases both the likelihood of having educational plans and of eventual attendance. These direct and indirect employment effects are strongest for women in the teaching and nursing professions.

The locational variables operate mainly indirectly by helping to fix a

Table 4–8
Weighted Probit Coefficients for Explanatory Variables in Reduced-Form Equations of College Attendance by 1967, Educational Plans in 1967, and College Attendance during 1968–1982

Variable Name[a]	Max. Likelihood Est. (Ratio of Est. to S.E.)		
	Attended College by 1967	Educational Plans, 1967	Attend College, 1968–1982
Origin status			
X_1 Hd. educ., yrs.	.1052 (11.56)*	.0069 (.89)	.0146 (1.61)
X_2 Hd. occ., Dun. SEI	.0111 (8.48)*	−.0002 (−.15)	.0026 (1.92)
X_3 Mother worked	−.1906 (−3.04)*	.0878 (1.74)	.0492 (.82)
X_4 Black	.1431 (1.28)	.5253 (5.95)*	−.0410 (−.35)
X_5 Age, 1967	−0.103 (−1.58)	−.0404 (−7.38)*	−.0165 (−2.26)*
X_6 H.S. acad.perf.	.2404 (14.71)*	.0454 (3.20)	.0990 (5.69)*
Location, 1967			
X_7 Residence (non-SMSA)			
City	—	.3642 (5.69)*	.0175 (.22)
Suburb	—	.2773 (4.61)*	.1031 (1.45)
X_8 South	—	−.1725 (−3.23)*	−.1850 (−2.85)*
X_9 Area unemp. rate	—	.0405 (3.21)*	.0375 (2.58)*
Labor market activity, early			
X_{10} Employed, 1963–1967 (none)			
Teaching	—	.9429 (7.28)*	.9175 (6.27)*
Nursing	—	.3300 (2.78)*	.9988 (7.56)*
Other prof., manag.	—	.1023 (.96)	.1800 (1.52)
Clerical, retail	—	.1978 (3.18)*	.2191 (3.01)*
Operative, craft.	—	.2326 (2.74)*	−.1088 (−.91)
Service, lab.	—	.1431 (1.75)	.0584 (.54)
Household characteristics			
X_{11} Health impaired, 1967	—	.0783 (1.19)	−.3619 (−3.98)*
X_{12} Hus. occ. 1967, Dun. SEI	—	.0045 (3.98)*	.0026 (2.02)*
X_{13} Marital status 1967, single	—	.1510 (2.19)*	.0620 (.62)
X_{14} Children, no. 1967	—	.0375 (2.88)*	.0107 (.51)
X_{15} Marital status ch.,			
67–72 (no ch.)			
New single	—	—	.1401 (1.12)
New married	—	—	−.1554 (−.81)
X_{16} Children, no inc. 67–72	—	—	−.0076) (−.21)
X_{17} Marital status ch.,			
73–77 (no ch.)			
New single	—	—	.0136 (.12)
New married	—	—	−.0246 (−.14)
X_{18} Children, no. inc. 72–77	—	—	−.0328 (−1.01)
Educational activity			
X_{19} Educ., yrs. attain. 1967	—	.1044 (7.66)*	.1725 (9.36)*
X_{21} Educ. plans 1967	—	—	.6636 (11.48)*
Constant	−3.028	−1.347	−3.677
Log likelihood ratio (−2)	789.59	577.87	1108.67
d.f.	6	21	28

Note: $N = 3,542$.

*p .05.

[a]See table 4–7 for variable definitions.

Table 4–9
Weighted Probit Coefficients for Explanatory Variables in Reduced-Form Equations of College Attendance during 1967–1972, 1972–1977, and 1977–1982

Variable Name[a]	Max. Likelihood Est. (Ratio of Est. to S.E.)					
	Coll. 67–72		Coll. 72–77		Coll. 77–82	
Origin status						
X_1 Hd. educ., yrs.	.0144	(1.26)	.0129	(1.29)	.0254	(2.69)*
X_2 Hd. occ., Dun. SEI	.0005	(.30)	.0022	(1.46)	.0014	(1.01)
X_3 Mother worked	−.0159	(−.20)	.0670	(1.00)	.0904	(1.43)
X_4 Black	−.1341	(−.87)	.1443	(1.11)	−.0049	(−.04)
X_5 Age, 1967	.0112	(1.29)	−.0041	(−.51)*	−.0180	(−2.34)*
X_6 H.S. acad.perf.	.0534	(2.31)*	.1038	(5.28)*	.0753	(4.15)*
Location, 1967						
X_7 Residence (non-SMSA)						
City	−.0681	(−.66)	.0020	(.02)	.0995	(1.19)
Suburb	−.0035	(.04)	.0862	(1.08)	.2305	(3.05)*
X_8 South	.0230	(.27)	−.2180	(−2.93)*	−.2294	(−3.29)*
X_9 Area unemp. rate	.0326	(1.81)	.0414	(2.62)	.0152	(.98)
Labor market activity, early						
X_{10} Employed, 1963–1967 (none)						
Teaching	.8040	(5.71)*	.5514	(4.14)*	.4554	(3.51)*
Nursing	.5231	(3.16)*	.7247	(5.24)*	1.0167	(7.73)*
Other prof., manag.	.2385	(1.60)	.1588	(1.20)	.1643	(1.30)
Clerical, retail	.1620	(1.61)	.1923	(2.30)*	.2044	(2.63)*
Operative, craft.	0.343	(.20)	−.0067	(−.05)	−.0915	(−.70)
Service, lab.	.2292	(1.55)	.0401	(.31)	.0413	(.35)
Household characteristics						
X_{11} Health impaired, 1967	−.2249	(−1.85)	−.2705	(−2.57)*	−.3356	(−3.41)*
X_{12} Hus. occ. 1967, Dun. SEI	−.0001	(−.08)	.0029	(1.96)*	.0042	(3.06)*
X_{13} Marital status 1967, single	.2335	(2.18)*	.0542	(.51)	.2020	(1.98)*
X_{14} Children, no. 1967	.0077	(.34)	.0217	(1.07)	.0518	(2.38)*
X_{15} Marital status ch., 67–72 (no ch.)						
New single	—		.1910	(1.54)	.1563	(1.18)
New married	—		−.1632	(−.75)	−.2827	(−1.38)
X_{16} Children, no inc. 67–72	—		.0047	(.12)	.0252	(.66)
X_{17} Marital status ch., 73–77 (no ch.)						
New single	—		—		.1203	(1.05)
New married	—		—		−.1454	(−.75)
X_{18} Children, no. inc. 72–77	—		—		.0039	(.12)
Educational activity						
X_{19} Educ., yrs. attain. 1967	.2060	(8.66)*	.1186	(5.78)*	.1244	(6.63)*
X_{21} Educ. plans 1967	.8408	(10.79)*	.3655	(5.54)*	.4580	(7.47)*
Constant	−5.493		−3,871		−3.329	
Log likelihood ratio (−2)	711.33		504.02		688.67	
d.f.	22		25		28	

Note: N = 3,542.

*p .05.

[a]See table 4–7 for variable definitions.

woman's educational plans, perhaps by delimiting her access to and awareness of available postsecondary institutions. Net of the other variables in the equation, plans are more likely if a woman lives outside the South, in a metropolitan area, and in an area of high unemployment. Region and area unemployment rate also have small direct effects on attendance.

The household characteristic variables in the main operated as expected, although somewhat weaker than the other variables in the model. The initial 1967 household characteristics did, however, have their expected significant effects. The most important variable was husband's occupational status, showing both positive direct effects on attendance and an indirect effect by plans. This variable was intended to index a family income effect, but it could also represent additional, more subtle social psychological processes. Interestingly, having many children in 1967 had positive effects on both plans and attendance during 1978–1982 although not on earlier attendance. It may be that the expectation of free time for study, in the subjective sense of a woman's having time on her hands, became more of a reality during this last time period for women who once had large families. The other family status variable—being single in 1967—also increased both the likelihood of having further plans and attendance during two of the three periods. These women also had more free time to expend in college study.

Most suggestive about the household change variables is the different operation of the "new single" variable in the education equations of tables 4–8 and 4–9 compared to the employment equation of table 4–10. The

Table 4–10
Weighted Probit Coefficients for Explanatory Variables in Reduced-Form Equations of Employment during 1977–1982

		Max. Likelihood Est. (Ratio of Est. to S.E.)	
Variable Name[a]		*Employed, 1977–1982*	
Origin status			
X_1	Hd. educ., yrs.	− .0037	(− 0.46)
X_2	Hd. occ., Dun. SEI	− .0020	(− 1.56)
X_3	Mother worked	.1913	(3.51)*
X_4	Black	− .1487	(− 1.57)
X_5	Age, 1967	− .0313	(− 4.98)*
X_6	H.S. acad.perf.	.0461	(3.11)*
Location, 1967			
X_7	Residence (non-SMSA)		
	City	− .0910	(− 1.39)
	Suburb	− .0917	(− 1.50)
X_8	South	− .0613	(− 1.12)
X_9	Area unemp. rate	− .0459	(− 3.52)*

Table 4–10 continued

Variable Name[a]	Max. Likelihood Est. (Ratio of Est. to S.E.)	
	Employed, 1977–1982	
Labor market activity, early		
X_{10} Employed, 1963–1967 (none)		
Teaching	.5192	(3.85)*
Nursing	.5813	(4.16)*
Other prof., manag.	.9527	(7.36)*
Clerical, retail	.7137	(10.68)*
Operative, craft.	.8060	(9.41)*
Service, lab.	.6901	(8.52)*
Household characteristics		
X_{11} Health impaired, 1967	−.3273	(−5.18)*
X_{12} Hus. occ. 1967, Dun. SEI	−.0023	(−1.92)
X_{13} Marital status 1967, single	.1443	(1.67)
X_{14} Children, no. 1967	.0063	(.36)
X_{15} Marital status ch.,		
67–72 (no ch.)		
New single	.3580	(2.96)*
New married	−.3078	(−1.90)
X_{16} Children, no inc. 67–72	.0268	(.92)
X_{17} Marital status ch.,		
73–72 (no ch.)		
New single	.2914	(2.78)*
New married	−.3733	(−2.42)*
X_{18} Children, no. inc. 72–77	−.0083	(−.29)
Educational activity		
X_{19} Educ., yrs. attain. 1967	.0168	(1.25)
X_{21} Educ. plans 1967	.1109	(1.90)
X_{26} Attend coll. 67–82,		
no. intervals	.2947	(6.47)*
Constant	1.295	
Log likelihood ratio (−2)	525.92	
d.f.	29	

Note: $N = 3,542$.
*p .05.
[a]See table 4–7 for variable definitions.

significant effect only in table 4–10 indicates that the household shock of losing a spouse is more likely to generate an employment response than an education response. The change score for number of children showed no effect in either the education or employment equations. Once variation in the initial level was included in the equation, the change score showed little variation, particularly for women in the same age cohort.

The employment equation in table 4–10, although not central to our focus, does show the strong effect that amount of adult college attendance has on increasing the likelihood of employment. Although many of the women who entered into adult college education may have done so purely for education's sake, there was a strong tendency for such women subsequently to enter employment. Whether their employment resulted from their increased human capital or perhaps from some new self-awareness gained from their education must await further inquiry. What is clear from this research is the increasingly widespread participation of women in formal adult education and the increasing tendency for this participation to be rooted in a lifelong educational career.

Notes

1. Table 4–1 contains insufficient degrees of freedom to disentangle possible age effects from the birth cohort and period effects noted in the text. With the appropriate cautions, however, one can interpret the apparent period cohort interaction as indicative of an underlying age effect. It may be that attendance rates increase over time more slowly in the earlier than in the later cohorts (2.5 point spread over the three time intervals, compared to an 8.8 point spread) because their older age makes them less sensitive to contemporary period effects. Their lower sensitivity, however, could also be a function of their lower attainment level. The other possibility is that the period effect at least in part reflects a more general aging of the U.S. population and the consequent freeing up of total time available for adult educational activity. Most of these women have not yet entered the age range when their age and associated ill health becomes an impediment to educational activity. Subsequent multivariate analyses better separate out period from age and cohort effects by explaining each respondent's attendance rates over the entire fifteen-year period and also within each five-year period and by including measures of age, health, and 1967 educational attainment level in the equations.

2. A more detailed equal-interval breakdown was not possible because of a paucity of educational data during the intermediate (1973–1977) years of the survey. The relatively great width of these periods and the arbitrary nature of their boundaries in relation to the life courses of the women thus call for caution in the use of these values.

3. The estimates to be presented are reduced-form estimates, in view of the fact that possible nonrecursive relationships among the education, household, and employment variables are not examined, nor is there any modeling of the error structure among the lagged endogenous variables representing attendance during the three time periods. Each of the attendance variables to be explained has a skewed, dichotomous distribution, and consequently all equations are estimated using maximum-likelihood weighted probit estimation. The sample used is the full cohort of 3,542 respondents available in 1982. As a check for possible selectivity bias due to attrition, separate OLS models of 1967 educational plans were estimated for the 1982 respondents ($N = 3,542$) and the original sample attriters ($N = 1,541$), using 1967 sample weights for the attriters. Of the twenty regression coefficients in the equation,

only six of the attriter coefficients had values more than two standard errors different from those in the 1982 respondent sample. Of these six, only three changed significance levels using the .05 criterion, with two of the attriter coefficients becoming nonsignificant (city residence and area unemployment rate) and one becoming significant (other professional employment). The overall stability of these estimates suggests that attrition bias should have negligible bearing on the generalizability of these findings to the original population cohort of mature women born between 1922 and 1936. These results are available upon request.

References

Bishop, J., and Van Dyk, J. 1977. "Can Adults Be Hooked on College?" *Journal of Higher Education* 48:39–62.

Hogan, D.P. 1978. "The Variable Order of Events in the Life Course." *American Sociological Review* 43:573–586.

Kline, C.M.; Livesy, H.B.; and Stern, M.R. 1975. "How to Tap the Adult Market." *College and University* 50:611–625.

Marini, M.M. 1983. "The Order of Events in the Transition to Adulthood." *Sociology of Education* 57:63–83.

Morgan, W.R. 1984. "The High School Dropout in an Overeducated Society." In P. Baker et al., *Pathways to the Future IV*. A Final Report on The National Longitudinal Surveys of Youth Labor Market Experience in 1982. Columbus, Ohio: Center for Human Resource Research, The Ohio State University.

National Center for Education Statistics. 1981. *Digest of Education Statistics*. Washington, D.C.: U.S. Government Printing Office.

Robinson, J.P. 1977. *How Americans Use Time*. New York: Praeger Press.

U.S. Bureau of the Census. 1984. Current Population Reports, Series P–20, No. 394. *School Enrollment–Social and Economic Characteristics of Students: October 1983*. Washington, D.C.: U.S. Government Printing Office.

5
Women's Labor Market Relations to Family Disruptions, Husband's Unemployment, or Husband's Disability

Donald R. Haurin

T he goal of this study is to measure the labor market response of married women to a variety of shocks to the household: husband's unemployment, husband's poor health, and marital disruption, including divorce, separation, or widowhood. The underlying model assumes that an unanticipated shock occurs at a point in time, and the wife's labor force response can be measured at a later date. Although the response may be immediate, it will also persist throughout the remaining life cycle of the family, implying that imbedded in any observation of the current supply of hours worked by the wife are her responses to prior shocks. The analysis aims to test whether the effects of prior shocks can be measured and to note any temporal changes in the size of the response.

Women's labor force responses will differ depending on the nature of the shock. The husband's unemployment will cause household income to fall and his quantity of time at home to increase. Additionally the husband may require nursing instead of being able to contribute by working around the house. Temporary and permanent health changes may also have different effects. The other shock variables measure marital disruption, where the husband is no longer present in the household. In the empirical analysis, the various types of marital disruption—divorce, separation, and widowhood—are each controlled for in an attempt to determine if the level or the time path of women's labor force response differs among these categories.

The Data

The first sample contains 1,220 observations of women who were married with a spouse present (MSP) in 1977. In table 5–1, some of the measures of household disruption are presented. For example, the first column reports the number of occurrences of health problems among husbands during the period

Table 5–1
Number of Observations of Households Suffering Shocks

Survey Years	Husband, Health Change	Husband, Permanently Disabled	Widowed	Divorced	Separated
1977–1979	80	30	27	10	25
1979–1981	100	36	19	7	8
1981–1982	78	–	14	6	12
Total	258	66	60	23	45

between the survey years listed. If the health problem persists over time and the husband does not work after reporting it, he is classified as permanently disabled. No husbands are coded as permanently disabled in 1981–1982 because of the short period of observation after the initial report. The cases of widowhood, separation, and divorce include only those who had not remarried by 1982.

Table 5–2 reports the percentage of husbands who experience some unemployment in the listed year and their mean number of weeks unemployed. In the empirical work, a threshold is imposed; the unemployment measure is set to 0 unless the sum of weeks unemployed is ten or more.

Table 5–3 summarizes the variation among households in the means of the variables measuring a woman's labor supply; the means and definitions of all variables used in the empirical analysis are presented in table 5–4. Of primary interest is the number of hours worked per year by the respondent (R-HOURS). The 1982 sample mean of this variable is 946 hours; the labor force participation rate for women (R-WORK) is 58.5 percent, and the mean number of hours per week (R-HR/WK) of working women is 34.6 hours.

Divorced and separated women work more hours per week and have higher labor force participation rates than the entire sample (table 5–3). The results are mixed for widowed women and wives whose husbands experience either a health problem or previous spells of unemployment. For women with husbands who became permanently disabled between 1977 and 1981, however, labor force participation is noticeably lower, and hours worked per week are slightly lower than sample means. The problem with attempting to

Table 5–2
Unemployment among Husbands

	1976	1979	1981	1982
Percentage unemployed	10.7	5.8	7.1	7.9
Mean weeks	22.4	15.4	17.9	18.0

Table 5–3
Mean of Respondent's Annual Hours Worked, Labor Force Participation Rate, and Typical Hours Worked per Week for Working Women

Survey	Husband, Health Change	Husband, Permanently Disabled	Widowed	Divorced	Separated
Respondent's annual hours worked, 1982 (R-HOURS)					
1977–1979	784	702	991	1,482	1,136
1979–1981	833	655	747	1,277	1,232
1981–1982	1,093	—	1,126	1,643	1,376
Respondent's labor force participation, 1982 (RWORK)					
1977–1979	.52	.47	.59	.90	.64
1979–1981	.56	.42	.58	.71	.63
1981–1982	.65	—	.71	.83	.75
Respondent's hours per week (working women), 1982 (R-HR/WK)					
1977–1979	33.1	30.9	36.3	37.3	38.9
1979–1981	32.0	34.1	27.9	39.6	39.4
1981–1982	36.0	—	33.2	40.1	40.4

	Husband Experiences Some Unemployment in Listed Year			
	1976	1979	1981	1982
Respondent's annual hours worked, 1982	1,025	748	1,111	835
Respondent's labor force participation, 1982	.62	.52	.66	.55
Respondent's hours per week, 1982	34.5	32.3	35.8	33.8

interpret the results in table 5–3 is that other factors affecting women's labor force behavior are not controlled for. The results of further empirical analysis, after controlling for these factors, are reported below. The formal labor model supply on which the empirical analysis is based may be found in appendix 5A.

Methodology

To test the proposition that women's current labor force behavior is affected by current and prior shocks to the family, a labor supply equation must be estimated. The model used here follows a common procedure, described in detail in Killingsworth's (1983) review of recent labor supply literature. The

Table 5–4
Variable Definitions and Means

Variable[a]	Definition	Mean
R-ED	Respondent's highest grade completed, reported in 1977	11.4
R-AGE	Respondent's age, 1982	52.0
R-HEALTH	Respondent's health prevents work, 1982, or limits the amount or kind of work, 1982	0.13
R-WAGE*	Respondent's hourly wage, NLS key variable, 1982	6.02
R-WEEKS*	Respondent's number of weeks worked, NLS key variable adjusted from between surveys to a 52-week period, 1982	46.0
R-HR/WK*	Respondent's number of usual hours worked per week, 1982	34.6
R-WORK	Dummy variable equaling 1 if wife worked in 1982	.59
R-EXP	Number of years respondent has worked 6 months or more prior to 1982; derived from a categorical variable	16.5
R-PEN/DIS	Respondent is pension or disability eligible	.12
R-HOURS	Respondent's annual hours worked, product of usual hours worked per week and number of weeks worked	945.9
H-WAGE*	Husband's hourly wage, derived as husband's wage or business income divided by annual hours worked	10.50
H-WORK	Dummy variable equaling 1 if husband worked in 1982	.71
H-HEALTH	Husband's health limits amount or kind of work, 1982	.23
H-HOURS	Husband's annual hours worked, product of usual hours worked per week and number of weeks worked	1446.2
WHITE	Dummy variable indicating respondent is white	.76
KIDS	Number of children aged 0 to 18 in household, 1982	.62
OTHERS	Number of household members aged 19 or older	.76
ASSETS	NLS key variable measuring asset level of household, in thousands of dollars	54.3
NORTH	Respondent's location is NORTH as defined in NLS handbook	.59
MEDIUM	Location in a medium-sized city; 50,000–499,999, based on 1979 Census of Population	.39
BIG	Location in a large city; 500,000 or more, based on 1979 Census of Population	.28
WID	Respondent was widowed between indicated years	—
DIV	Respondent was divorced between indicated years	—
SEP	Respondent was separated between indicated years	—
HLCH	Husband developed health problem in indicated years	—
HPD	Husband became permanently disabled in indicated years	—
H-UP	Sum of husband's weeks unemployed in indicated years, set to 0 if less than 10 weeks	—

Note: Universe: Married, spouse present in 1977, nonfarm families. Responses reported for all variables. There were no remarriages. Sample size, 1,220.

[a]An asterisk indicates the mean is for workers only.

end product is a Tobit estimation of the respondent's annual hours worked.[1] In the hours equation are explanatory factors, including the shock measures, assets, respondent's health, variables such as number of children that may affect the value of the respondent's time spent in the home, and estimates of the women's and husband's potential wages. These wage estimates are made in two ways. The first uses equations estimating the respondent's and husband's wages in 1982 for all persons with wages in that year.[2] The second uses estimates based on three years—1979, 1981, and 1982—for people who worked in all three years. This latter method has the advantage that unobserved individual characteristics such as special abilities, attitudes, and work habits that may affect wages can be taken into account indirectly.

Results

Cross-Sectional Wage Measure

Two sets of Tobit results are presented. The first (table 5–5) is the hours equation that includes temporal disaggregated measures of the family disruptions. In this framework, the adjustments to shocks, both recent and up to five years prior, can be estimated, but the disaggregation makes the number of respondents suffering shocks in each period relatively small (see table 5–1). Table 5–6 presents the results with the shocks aggregated to single measures for the 1977–1982 period, thus facilitating comparisons with the analysis based on the alternative wage measure.

The results presented in table 5–5 indicate that marital disruption significantly increases the number of hours of work in the cases of divorce and separation and moderately increases them in widowhood. The total effect of the loss of a husband is the sum of the coefficient of the appropriate dummy variable and the effect created by the loss of the husband's wage.[3] However, the coefficient of the natural log of husband's wage is only 39 with a *t* value of 0.4; thus the contribution of the loss of the husband's wage is small and statistically insignificant.[4]

In terms of the magnitude of the change in hours, the more recent is the divorce or separation, the larger is the change in hours. Also the effect of a separation is less than a divorce, averaging about two-thirds the amount for comparably timed shocks. The implication is that these two types of marital disruption have lasting effects on a woman's labor force behavior, and the largest change occurs just after the loss of the husband.[5]

The effects of changing husband's health on the wife's labor supply are determined by inspecting a series of coefficients. If the husband had a health problem that occurred before 1977 and persisted until 1982, the wife's annual hours of work increase by 98. If a health problem developed between

Table 5–5
Tobit Estimates of Women's Hours of Work, 1982

			Dependent	*R-Hours*	
R-ED	143.8	(3.9)	WID7779	289.5	(1.3)
(R-ED)^2	– 17.7	(10.5)	WID7981	127.6	(0.5)
NORTH	147.0	(3.1)	WID8182	159.9	(0.6)
MEDIUM	– 464.0	(9.0)	DIV7779	619.5	(2.3)
BIG	– 1172.3	(18.9)	DIV7981	719.9	(2.4)
R-HEALTH	– 338.0	(6.5)	DIV8182	1035.4	(3.3)
H-HEALTH	97.6	(1.6)	SEP7779	282.5	(1.5)
R-PEN/DIS	– 372.4	(5.5)	SEP7981	576.3	(2.0)
R-EXP*	– 17.5	(2.1)	SEP8182	660.2	(2.7)
KIDS	44.5	(1.1)	HLCH7779	– 246.4	(2.4)
OTHERS	136.6	(6.5)	HLCH7981	– 64.9	(0.7)
WHITE	– 45.8	(0.7)	HLCH8182	65.6	(0.7)
ASSETS	– 1.7	(4.5)	HPD7779	– 193.2	(1.1)
CONSTANT	– 5265.3	(16.4)	HPD7981	– 438.0	(2.7)
ln H-WAGE	39.1	(0.4)	H-UP7679	2.9	(1.4)
ln R-WAGE	4068.6	(41.2)	H-UP8182	6.5	(2.8)

Note: In all tables in this chapter, the numbers in parentheses are *t* statistics.

Table 5–6
Abbreviated List of Coefficient Estimates for a Tobit Analysis of Work Hours for Women

			Dependent	*R-HOURS*	
WID7782	253.7	(1.4)	H-HEALTH	150.8	(2.6)
DIV/SEP7782	617.5	(3.6)	HLCH7782	– 120.3	(2.0)
ln H-WAGE*	62.0	(0.6)	HDD7781	– 392.7	(3.7)
ln R-WAGE*	4061.0	(42.1)	H-UP7682	2.2	(1.8)

Notes: $N = 1,220$.
*The shocks are temporally aggregated.

1977 and 1979 and persisted until 1982 but did not prevent the husband from working, the net effect is that the wife's labor supply is lower by 148 hours. The estimate of the effect of a recent (1981–1982) decline in husband's health is an increase of 163 hours of work. If the decline in husband's health is permanent and he does not work, the estimated effect is more substantial. The total effect of the husband's acquiring a permanent disability between the 1979 and 1981 surveys is a reduction in the wife's labor supply by 405 hours (– 438 – 65 + 98). If the health change occurred between

1977 and 1979, the total effect is a reduction of hours by 341 (-193 – 246 + 98). Permanent changes in husband's health result in a persistent reduction in the wife's labor supply. One interpretation is that a severe health problem induces the wife to stay home to take care of her husband.

The final set of variables measuring shocks to a household are the unemployment measures for the husband. Only spells of unemployment of at least 2.5 months in a two-year period are included as determinants of women's labor supply, and the period of unemployment need not be continuous. The wife's estimated response is an increase of 6.5 annual hours per week of husband's unemployment if the unemployment was relatively recent but an increase of only 2.9 hours annually if the spells of unemployment were at least three years earlier (the latter result if only marginally significant). These results generally confirm two predictions of our model. First, a woman's supply of labor will increase if the husband's labor supply is rationed at a level below that which was planned. Second, the response of the wife will not be a temporary increase in hours worked that would completely offset the husband's shortfall; the response will instead be maintained through the remaining planning period.

Other results contained in table 5–5 are of interest: the near-zero effect of the husband's wage on wife's hours (cross-wage effect), the statistically significant but numerically small effect of asset levels, and the large coefficient of the respondent's own wage. With assets measured in thousands of dollars, a substantial increase in assets of $50,000 results in a decline in women's labor supply by only 85 hours.[6] The effect of the respondent's own wage is large, the coefficient of ln-R-WAGE being 4,068.6. Given that the woman is working, the change in her expected hours of work in response to changes in the log of own wage is 3,511.[7] Starting from this figure, we can calculate the wage elasticity of labor supply, a commonly used measure of responsiveness of hours worked to a change in wages. Wage elasticities of 1 or above indicate that hours worked are very responsive to the available wage. Mean hours of work by working women is 1,603, yielding an estimated wage elasticity of labor supply, conditional on being in the labor force, of 2.19 (3411/1603). Prior cross-sectional measures have ranged widely, from near 0 to well above 4 (Killingsworth 1983, pp. 195–199).[8]

Table 5–6 shows the results of a Tobit analysis in which the shock measures are aggregated across the five years. Generally, the results are similar to those reported for the temporally disaggregated shock measures.

In summary, marital disruption increases the number of hours a woman supplies to the labor force, the largest effect occurring with a divorce, the next largest effect with separation, and a smaller (marginally significant) effect with widowhood. For divorce and separation, the size of the effect is largest for recent occurrences. The results also suggest that a husband's recent unemployment directly increases the wife's labor supply at a rate of 6 hours annually per week of husband's unemployment. An indirect effect of unemployment could occur through asset levels, but the estimated effect of a change in assets upon labor supply is small.

The other series of household disruption variables measure changes in the husband's health. If the husband acquires a health problem that is not severe, the wife's labor supply is basically unchanged, but if his problem is severe, her reduction in hours is significant.

Longitudinally Based Wage Measure

Next we discuss the results of employing a different methodology to estimate male and female wage rates, retaining the cross-sectional framework for the empirical analysis. Survey data from 1982, 1981, and 1979 are used to generate a wage estimate that allows for the inclusion of usually unmeasured factors that affect a specific person's wage.[9] Following the method used in the prior analysis, the new wage measures are estimated and used in a Tobit analysis of women's labor supply.[10] These yield results that can be compared to those presented in table 5–6. One problem encountered with this approach is that the data requirements are stricter and 350 observations are dropped because of the lack of data in 1979 or 1981. A new sample of 870 respondents is the basis for the equations. Because the number of households reporting shocks declines more than proportionally, temporal aggregation of the shock variables is required.[11]

The new Tobit results in table 5–7 reveal a number of notable differences when they are compared to the results in table 5–6, particularly for the wage variables. The coefficient of ln H-WAGE changes from near zero to – 410, while that of ln R-WAGE drops substantially to 1,466. The effect of a marital disruption must be interpreted with some care now that the husband's wage coefficient is significantly different from 0. Losing a husband with average wage implies that hours of work rise by $(-410) \times (-2.35) = 964$. Therefore the total effects of divorce, separation, and widowhood are increases of 856 hours, 898 hours, and 419 hours, respectively. Compared to the results in table 5–6, the new approach suggests somewhat larger responses to separation and widowhood, while the estimated response to divorce is quite similar.

A woman's labor market response to the husband's acquiring a health problem is small, but, as before, the change is large if the husband becomes permanently disabled (a 316 hour decrease). If the husband has a longstanding health problem that does not prevent his working, the wife's hours worked show a significant increase of 221 hours. Her estimated response to her husband's unemployment is now 7 hours for each week of his unemployment, somewhat larger than before.

The new wage estimates are not generated by the change in sample size.[12]

Table 5–7
Tobit Estimates of Hours Worked by Women, 1982, Using Wage
Measures That Include Individual Effects

			Dependent	*R-Hours*	
R-ED	162.6	(3.3)	WHITE	198.2	(2.3)
(R-ED)^2	– 3.1	(1.5)	ASSETS	– 2.4	(5.6)
NORTH	– 75.0	(1.2)	CONSTANT	– 1417.7	(3.3)
MEDIUM	– 18.2	(0.3)	ln R-WAGE	1465.9	(15.4)
BIG	– 378.9	(5.7)	ln H-WAGE	– 409.6	(5.4)
R-HEALTH	– 814.4	(10.6)	WID7782	– 544.8	(3.1)
H-HEALTH	220.9	(3.3)	DIV7782	– 107.8	(0.5)
P-PEN/DIS	– 161.1	(2.2)	SEP7782	– 65.7	(0.3)
R-EXP	– 35.1	(2.9)	HLCH7782	– 13.8	(0.2)
KIDS	– 39.5	(0.8)	HPD7781	– 525.0	(4.0)
OTHERS	48.6	(1.8)	H-UP7679	7.1	(4.9)

If the cross-sectional equations are used to generate wage rates for the longitudinal sample, the coefficient of ln R-WAGE returns to a high level (6,454), and that ln H-WAGE becomes positive (292). The conclusion is that the reduction in the estimated response of women to variations in their own wage is due to the new method of estimating wages rather than to the reduction in sample size. Similarly the significantly negative cross-wage effect is also due to the change in method, not the change in sample size.

One other variation was tried that relaxed the constraint imposed by the functional form of the labor supply equation. The association between a woman's labor supply and the level of the husband's wage is determined by the entire sample. The functional form imposes the assumption that the response to a change in husband's potential wage is the same as the response that occurs if the marriage is disrupted and the husband is no longer present. A less constrained approach is to add an interaction variable between the log of husband's wage and a dummy variable equaling 1 if the woman is widowed, divorced, or separated.[13] Although more freedom is now allowed in the determination of the responses to marital disruption, the estimates remain about the same. At mean husband's wage, the increases in women's hours are 967 for divorce, 1,009 for separation, and 629 for widowhood.

The wage elasticity estimates during the longitudinal wage measure differ from those derived from the cross-sectional wage. Conditional on the woman's being in the labor force, her own wage elasticity is estimated to be 1.04, and the cross-wage elasticity estimate is – 0.29. Finally, the asset measure is now significant as well. It appears that the use of a more adequate wage measure reduces the importance of the woman's own wage and increases the importance of other family income and some of the shock variables.

Conclusion

Different types of household disruptions are likely to lead to different responses in women's labor supply. Substantial responses are noted for marital disruption—an estimated increase in the women's work time of about 900 hours for divorce and somewhat fewer than 900 hours for a separation. The response to widowhood is also an increase in hours of work, but the magnitude is not estimated very precisely (in the range of 100–600 hours). If the husband acquires a health problem that is not severe enough to prohibit further work, the wife's labor supply remains at the original level or increases slightly. If the husband's disability is permanent—if he does not return to work in the sample period—the wife's hours of work decline by 100–500 hours annually. Finally, if the husband was recently unemployed, the cross-sectional evidence using the larger sample indicates that the wife increases her labor supply at a rate of 6 hours annually for each week of her husband's unemployment. Estimates of a working woman's elasticity of labor supply with respect to her own wage were about 2.0 for the cross-sectional wage measure and 1.0 for the longitudinal measure. The estimate of the elasticity of her labor supply with respect to her husband's wage is small, the preferred estimate being about − .25.

The estimates indicate that a woman's labor supply response is nearly immediate; little or no time is spent in training or further education. Because the analysis is based on a cohort of women with an average age of 52 years, the quick responses are consistent with human capital models of labor supply. If the analysis were of much younger women, the human capital models would predict that women would engage in relatively more training activities after suffering a shock to the family.

This study supports the proposition that the number of hours worked by a woman depends on the wage she is able to earn in the marketplace and her family environment. Sudden and unexpected changes to her household disrupt her planned labor force activities, and the evidence suggests that she responds quickly in a manner that stabilizes the household's income. If her husband suffers long bouts of unemployment, she increases her supply of labor by a moderate amount. If he becomes permanently disabled, however, she is more likely to decrease her hours of work, perhaps because of the need to provide care for him. If her husband is not longer present because of a divorce or separation, her labor supply increases by a substantial amount.

Appendix 5A   A Model of a Woman's Response to an Unanticipated Shock to the Husband's Employment

Consider a model where lifetime utility is maximized. In each period the husband and wife select the amount of labor they will supply and the quantity of goods they will purchase. This optimization is made subject to a lifetime budget constraint where income is derived from the husband's and wife's earnings and the returns from the stock of assets. The result of this optimization is a series of time-dependent demand equations for leisure and goods. These equations specify the intertemporal optimal paths of labor supply.

Into this framework introduce an unexpected shock to the husband's labor supply in a particular period. The family can start its adjustment immediately by replanning the woman's supply of labor and changing the quantity of goods consumed. Even if the shock is of relatively short duration, the new optimal paths will generally differ from the original plan for the entire remainder of the planning period. Short-term shocks are expected to have lasting, but moderate, effects on a woman's supply of labor. Because the rationing is assumed to reduce a husband's work hours, the lifetime full income of the family is reduced. Given that leisure is typically found to be a normal good (the demand for leisure rises with increased exogenous family income), a woman's response to a shock would be to reduce her demand for leisure or, equivalently, increase the supply of labor in the following periods. The model suggests that the deviation in her hours of work from the preshock optimal path will be directly related to the size of the shock. Also her tendency to increase work hours will be greatest in periods where the wage offered is relatively high.

If the model is further generalized to include a series of shocks to the husband's supply of labor, then the wife's work hours after the latest shock deviate from the preshock optimal path in a manner directly related to the cumulative discounted monetary loss to the family attributable to the shocks. The woman's current supply of labor is affected by those factors that typically influence her supply of labor, but it is modified by past shocks to the family; that is labor data reflect not only her current circumstances but also include current responses to prior events. Thus insights into a woman's labor supply elasticity may be derived from a cross-sectional estimation.

A mathematical model that allows for substitution between men's and women's labor supply within a period but limits intertemporal response to be based on income effects only is presented in Haurin (1985).

Notes

1. The Tobit model is used because positive hours of work are only observed if the woman works; otherwise zero hours are registered. One advantage of the Tobit

method is that it includes both workers and nonworkers. This method also takes into account both the participation and the hours supplied decisions, and it uses information about the number of hours worked by those who work. Discussions of the Tobit model are contained in many sources (for example, Judge et al. 1985, pp. 780–785). The LIMDEP statistical package is used for the estimation.

2. The wage estimates are derived from regressions on the working population only (Heckman 1979). First, probit analyses of the participation decisions were executed, including as explanatory variables the determinants of the market wages, the determinants of the reservation wages, exogenous income, and the shock measures. Next, a variable (inverse Mill's ratio) was generated for each of the workers in the sample. This variable was then included in a second wage regression, which also included other explanatory variables, such as education and measures of training. Estimates of wages corrected for selectivity bias were created for women and their husbands, and these measures were then employed in the Tobit analysis of annual hours. Tables detailing the estimates of the background participation and wage equations are available from the author.

3. The husband's wage is zero only if there is no husband present; otherwise a measure of the potential wage is included. An alternative interpretation of this procedure is that the model suggests that a woman's labor supply is only influenced by ln H-WAGE if a husband is present in the household. Setting ln H-WAGE to zero if the husband is absent eliminates the cross-wage effect and models the labor supply of a single woman.

4. The point estimate is 39* Δ (ln H-WAGE). If the husband earned the average wage, the value of Δ (ln H-WAGE) is − 2.35 implying a decrease of 92 work hours. This effect nearly offsets the positive coefficients of WID7981 and WID8182.

5. The universe excludes remarried women.

6. Asset levels are included rather than a measure of exogenous income because items such as the imputed rental value of an owned home are not included in the flow measure. Given some rate of return to assets, say 10 percent, the variables can be interpreted as measuring the flow of nonlabor income (in hundreds of dollars). See Killingsworth (1983, pp. 109–110) for a further summary.

7. To calculate the conditional response, see Judge et al. (1985, p. 784).

8. Also notable in table 5–5 are the large coefficients of the city size variable. These estimates are sensitive to the methodology used to create the wage variables. The wage variable is a 1982 measure, but it is nominal in the sense that it is not deflated to account for regional and urban variations in wages. Urban theory and empirical work has established that in a competitive model with utility-maximizing mobile laborers, wages will vary with city size because the cost of living is higher in large cities. This effect is found in both men's and women's wage equation estimates with the coefficient of BIG being .279 and that of MEDIUM equaling .109 in the respondent's wage equation. (Given the lack of specific locational data for the older women's cohort, it is not possible to estimate a deflated wage equation). Hours supplied are a function of real wages; thus the city size variables are also entered into the hours analysis, which explains the large size of their coefficients. For example, living in a large city raises the log of the respondent's nominal wage by .279, leading to an indirect increase in labor supply of 4068.6 * .279 = 1,135 hours; but the direct effect

(the coefficient of BIG) is $-1,172$ yielding a net effect of only -37 hours annually. Similarly, the indirect and direct effects of living in midsized cities are $4,068 * .109 = 443$ and -464, yielding a net effect of only -21 annual hours. Finally, the direct and indirect effects of living in the north are $4,068.6* (-.029) = -118$ and 147, yielding a small net effect of a 29 hour increase.

9. In this wage equation, it is assumed that the error structure includes a mean zero error specific to individuals, an error specific to a time period, and a purely random component that fluctuates over time and people. See Judge et al. (1985, pp. 515–538) for a thorough discussion of the error components model and a comparison with the fixed effects model. This assumption is appropriate if the individual specific errors are not correlated with the explanatory factors. If this assumption does not hold, then the estimated coefficients in the wage equation are biased.

For a particular person the best linear unbiased estimate of their wage is (Taub 1979):

$$w_{it} = a_j X_{ijt} + b_i \bar{e}_i,$$

where X_j is a vector of explanatory variables that varies over people (indexed as i) and time; the a_j and b_i are derived from a time series cross-sectional (TSCS) regression; $\bar{e}_j$ is the mean of an individual's residual in the wage regression; and finally,

$$b_i = Ts_d^2 / (s_n^2 + Ts_d^2).$$

The number of periods is T, which is three in this case. The variance estimates, s_d and s_n, are generated by the TSCS regression.

10. Issues related to selectivity bias and censoring are agin encountered, similar to those present in the cross-sectional analysis. In the wage equations, the selectivity variables are generated as follows. For both men and women, the sample is separated into those who worked each year (1979, 1981, 1982) and the remainder of the observations. Probit analyses of factors affecting the probability of working in all three years are then estimated for men and women. The matching of the time period of the dependent variable (a single measure for a three-year period) and the explanatory factors (separate data for each of three years) poses a problem. The 1981 values were selected for use in the participation regression. From the probits, selectivity variables are calculated for both men and women and they are retained for use in the wage equations.

11. Sample size falls by 28.7 percent; the reduction in the disruption measures are 43.5 percent, divorced; 42.2 percent, separated; 28.7 percent, husband's health changed, 28.3 percent, widowed; 27.3 percent, permanently disabled. The number of observations of husbands suffering unemployment greater than ten weeks in a two-year period falls by 19.4 percent for 1976 and 1979 and by 31.9 percent for 1981 and 1982.

12. The 1982 variable's means in the 870 sample are quite similar to the means in the 1,220 sample. Among the important variables, differences are noted in the following cases. In the smaller sample, NORTH is 8 percent higher, R-HOURS is 4 percent higher, H-HOURS is 3 percent lower, ASSETS are 4 percent higher, and

WHITE is 5 percent higher. The unemployment rate for husbands is 14.1 percent in 1976 rather than the 10.7 percent observed in the larger sample.

13. Because a 1982 value for ln H-WAGE is not calculated if the husband is absent, the predicted 1979 value of ln H-WAGE is substituted.

References

Berger, Mark C. 1983. "Labor Supply and Spouse's Health: The Effects of Illness, Disability, and Mortality." *Social Science Quarterly* 64:494–509.

Berger, Mark C., and Fleisher, Belton M. 1984. "Husband's Health and Wife's Labor Supply." *Journal of Health Economics* 3:63–75.

Greene, William. 1979. "Sample Selection Bias as a Specification Error: Comment." *Econometrica* 47:153–161.

Haurin, Donald R. 1985. "Women's Labor Market Reactions to Family Disruptions, Husband's Unemployment or Disability." In L.B. Shaw, ed., *Dual Careers*. Vol. 6. Columbus: Center for Human Resource Research, The Ohio State University.

Heckman, James J. 1979. "Sample Selection Bias as a Specification Error." *Econometrica* 47:153–161.

Judge, G.G.; Griffith, W.E., R.C.; Lugkepohl, H.; and Lee, T. 1985. *The Theory and Practice of Econometrics*. 2d ed. New York: John Wiley.

Killingsworth, M. 1983. *Labor Supply*. Cambridge: Cambridge University Press.

Taub, A.J. 1979. "Prediction in the Context of the Variance Components Model." *Journal of Econometrics* 10:103–108.

6
Early Labor Market Withdrawal

Robert J. Gitter
Lois B. Shaw
Mary G. Gagen

I n the period after midlife but before the age of 60, most women no longer
have young children in the home, so the major work-family conflict that
looms so large in most discussions of women's labor supply decisions is
less applicable. At this point, new factors such as the support of children in
college and health problems, of both the women themselves and other family
members, may assume greater importance. Given that family constraints are
less binding, it would be of interest to determine what factors influence
employed women to stop working.

The mature women's cohort of the NLS provides an excellent source of
data to study the causes of this phenomenon. The sample analyzed consists of
women who reported at least one week of employment during the year previous to the 1977 survey; they are considered to have withdrawn from the
labor market if they reported they had not worked in the year prior to the
1982 survey.[1] Hence this study examines the determinants of stopping work
by 1982 for mature women who reported some employment in 1977.[2]

Model of Labor Market Withdrawal

The influences chosen to examine may be grouped into four broad categories:
prior labor market commitment and success, current family needs and
resources, the health of the woman and other members of her household, and
the current condition of the local labor market.

We expect that the greater is a woman's commitment and success in the
labor force in 1977, the more likely she is to be employed five years hence.
The hourly rates of pay that the women earned in 1977 are an indication of
the success the women enjoyed earlier. Further, her 1977 pay rate serves as a
proxy for the wage rate she could have expected to earn in 1982.[3] The degree
of commitment to work is measured by the number of weeks worked out of
the fifty-two weeks prior to the 1977 survey week. The greater the number of
weeks she worked in 1977, the greater is the commitment to work and hence
a smaller probability of not working.

Family obligations and financial support are also likely to influence a woman's decision to stop working. The greater is the level of family income, independent of the woman's contribution, the less financial need there is for the woman to work and therefore a greater probability of her stopping work. Moreover, greater family income might enable her to enjoy her leisure more.

In addition to the effect of the absolute level of family income, changes in family income should influence decisions about work. Families become accustomed to specific levels of income, and changes in these accustomed levels could have an impact on a woman's decision to leave the labor market. A woman whose husband's annual income rose from $10,000 to $20,000 between 1977 and 1982 might be more likely to stop working than a woman whose husband earned $20,000 each year.

Family size should also bear on whether a woman stops working. Other things being equal, a larger family has greater financial needs. Therefore we would expect women in larger families to continue working. There is no need to expect that the effect of additional family members on the decision to keep working need be the same for all types of family members. Some dependents require personal care; others need financial assistance. We attempt to take these differences into account by examining the effect of three different types of family members on the decision to leave paid employment. Because some women choose to continue working to help finance their children's college education, we have constructed a measure of the number of dependent children enrolled in college. We also take into account potential financial need by including the number of nondependent children in college. Finally, the total number of dependents in the household excluding college students is included as the conventional measure of demands for her home time, which competes with her working. The health of the woman and her family should also play a part in her decision to remain at work. We have constructed two measures of her health to include in the model. The first is an index that measures how well the woman can accomplish each of thirteen different activities.[4] The potential values of the index range between 0 and 26, with the higher values representing greater degrees of physical impairment. The second index measures how many of eight health-related symptoms the woman reports.[5] We expect that a limited ability to perform common activities and a greater number of medical problems should be associated with a woman's withdrawing from the labor market.

The health enjoyed by other members of the household is a related factor. The health problems of another member of the household could create additional expenses, increasing the probability the woman will continue to work. On the other hand, the additional personal care required for a family member in ill health could provide an incentive for the woman to stop working and provide the needed care herself. A woman who reports that the health of any family members restricts her own work is given a value of 1 for this variable; all others have a value of 0.

The final category is condition of the local labor market. High levels of unemployment increase the probability that a woman might lose a job. Furthermore, the poor condition of the labor market will make it more difficult for her to find employment if she quits or loses a job. As a result, high levels of community unemployment should increase the likelihood that a woman stops working.[6]

We expect each of these factors to have an impact on a woman's decision to keep working. Their effect need not be the same for all groups, however. To examine their effect on different age, race, and marital status groups, separate logit equations were estimated for the various categories. We first estimated equations on the 451 nonwhite and 1,116 white women who were employed in 1977. All of the employed women for whom data are available are included in these equations. We also perform separate logit analyses for white women aged 45–49, 50–54, and 55–59 to examine the effects of the variables by age group. Finally, the model is estimated by race for women who are married with their husband present in the household.

Description of the Women in the Sample

Table 6–1 provides descriptive information, with separate means for each subgroup. The means are weighted to give a better picture of the population of women in this age group. Overall 14.5 percent of the women who had some employment in 1977 had withdrawn by 1982. The chances of withdrawing increased with age from 12.0 percent for the 45–49 group to 17.6 percent for the group aged 55–59. Married white women were more likely to stop working than white women in general. This relationship was reversed for nonwhite women, however, with married women being less likely to stop working. In general, older women and nonwhite women had lower levels of other family income, fewer college-enrolled dependents, and more physical limitations and symptoms than their younger white counterparts. Differences in the mean values of other variables were not as dramatic.

Determinants of Labor Market Withdrawal

Logit results for whites and nonwhites are presented in table 6–2. The dependent variable is withdrawal from the labor market, which is coded 1 for withdrawal and 0 for continuing to work. The equations were run in an unweighted logit form.[7]

The results for whites generally confirmed our hypotheses. The greater a woman's prior commitment to the labor market, the more likely she was to continue working. The more weeks a woman worked in 1977, the more likely she was to be employed in 1982. However, her wage rate in 1977, a

Table 6–1
Characteristics of the Women in the Samples

Variable	Nonwhite	White	Whites			Nonwhite MSP[a]	White MSP[a]
			Aged 45–49	Aged 50–54	Aged 55–59		
Withdrew from labor force[b]	15.1	14.4	12.0	13.3	17.6	12.9	16.3
Hourly rate of pay, 1977	5.73	6.27	6.03	6.31	6.45	5.60	6.02
Weeks worked, 1977	46.7	46.4	44.6	46.7	47.6	46.3	46.0
Other family income, 1981[c]	7.72	16.0	18.5	16.6	13.0	12.4	20.9
Change in husband's income (1976–1981)[c]	−2.12	−2.54	−1.25	−2.75	−3.55	−2.10	−2.13
Number of dependents in college	.18	.23	.35	.23	.11	.23	.27
Number of nondependent children	.09	.16	.17	.19	.13	.08	.16
Number of other dependents	.85	.50	.82	.47	.23	1.05	.54
Index of physical impairment	1.89	1.59	1.25	1.32	2.17	1.58	1.46
Number of symptoms	1.07	.64	.53	.53	.84	.82	.55
Other family member in ill health[b]	.05	.04	.03	.03	.05	.09	.04
Local unemployment rate	7.94	7.79	7.79	7.90	7.71	7.91	7.85
Number of observations	451	1,116	375	348	393	212	801

Note: All values are weighted means except for number of observations.
[a]Married spouse present.
[b]1 = yes; 0 = no.
[c]In thousands, 1981 dollars.

Table 6–2
Logit Analysis of Labor Market Withdrawal, by Race

Independent Variable	Nonwhite		White	
Intercept	−.798	(−0.94)	−1.93***	(−4.19)
Hourly rate of pay, 1977	−.181**	(−2.07)	−.027	(−0.70)
Weeks worked, 1977	−.053***	(−4.94)	−.040***	(−5.86)
Other family income, 1981[a]	.039*	(1.77)	.052***	(6.29)
Change in husband's income (1976–1981)[a]	−.033	(−1.48)	−.002	(−0.31)
Number of dependent children in college	−.582	(−1.23)	−.922***	(−3.34)
Number of nondependent children in college	.146	(0.26)	−.101	(0.40)
Number of other dependents	−.183	(−1.39)	−.444***	(−3.22)
Index of physical impairment	.218***	(−1.39)	.133***	(4.62)
Number of symptoms	.133	(1.26)	.340***	(5.00)
Other family member in ill health	.928	(1.46)	1.07***	(2.69)
Local unemployment rate	.121**	(2.03)	.105***	(3.27)
Number of observations	451		1,116	
−2 Log of likelihood function	240.81		702.06	

Note: Numbers in parentheses are the asymptotic t-ratios.

[a]In thousands, 1981 dollars.

***Significant at .01 level.

**Significant at .05 level.

*Significant at .10 level.

measure of her success at that time and a proxy for her wage rate in 1982 as well, was not significant.

The effects of family size and resources were generally as expected. Additional dependents, in college or not, decreased the probability of a woman's stopping work. The impact of having a dependent in college seemed to have about twice the effect of having other dependents on a woman's continuing to work (a coefficient of −.922 compared to −.444); this stronger effect is probably due to the greater level of income needed to maintain a child in college. In addition, although the presence of children under college age may increase a woman's need to work, the fact that younger children need more care may serve as a countervailing force to her remaining in the work force. Nondependent college students did not have a significant effect on the decision to withdraw from the labor market. Greater levels of family income, exclusive of a woman's earnings, led to a greater chance of her stopping work; that is, the greater the ability of a family to maintain a given standard of living independent of a woman's financial contribution, the less likely she was to work. Changes in the level of her husband's income did not have a statistically significant effect on her decision to stop working.

The two measures of a woman's health also had the predicted effect. A greater degree of physical impairment and a greater number of medical complaints each result in a greater chance of a woman's stopping work. Although the effect of having another family member with a health problem was ambiguous a priori, the results indicate that the presence of a person in the household with a health problem makes it more likely that a woman will stop working outside the home.

The final group of factors, the local labor market condition, shows that a higher level of unemployment is associated with a greater probability of a woman's withdrawing from the labor market. If there are relatively few job opportunities in the local labor market, she is more likely to stop working.[8]

For nonwhites, labor market success and commitment play a larger role in the decision to work than for whites. Hourly rate of pay has a statistically significant impact on the decision to withdraw for nonwhites but not for whites. The number of weeks worked in 1977 has a significant impact for both races, but the effect is a quarter larger for nonwhites. Nonwhites are less sensitive to family size and resource factors than whites. Although the level of physical disability has a greater effect on nonwhites, the number of symptoms has a greater effect on whites. A family's ill health affected only whites, while the impact of the unemployment rate was similar for both races.

Determinants for Married Women

Since the results reported for labor market withdrawal might have been confounded by the correlation of marital status with other factors, the model is reestimated for both races on a sample of married women. Although logit equations for groups with different marital status would have been of interest, the analysis was confined to married women because of the small number of women among the other marital status groups. The model was estimated separately by race (see table 6–3).

The picture that emerges for married women is similar to the one for the sample as a whole. With one exception, the logit results were quite similar for the two groups in terms of the magnitudes and statistical significance of the coefficients. Only the hourly rate of pay had a markedly different effect, taking on a smaller coefficient and losing significance in the equation for nonwhite married women.[9]

Nonwhite married women are less likely to stop working than their white counterparts, and in general, their continued labor market activity seems less sensitive to changes in the factors included in the model. The amount of family income, number of dependents of any status, number of physical

Table 6–3
Logit Analysis of Labor Market Withdrawal for Married Women

Independent Variable	Nonwhite		White	
Intercept	−.918	(−0.77)	−1.79***	(−3.41)
Hourly rate of pay, 1977	−.012	(−0.11)	−.043	(−1.00)
Weeks worked, 1977	−.073***	(−4.60)	−.035***	(−4.45)
Other family income, 1981[a]	.043	(1.37)	.043***	(4.30)
Change in husband's income (1976–1981)[a]	−.039	(−1.49)	−.004	(−0.53)
Number of dependent children in college	−.556	(−0.80)	−.834***	(−3.04)
Number of nondependent children in college	.021	(0.23)	−.053	(0.20)
Number of other dependents	−.084	(−0.48)	−.360***	(−2.55)
Index of physical impairment	.194**	(2.04)	.140***	(3.98)
Number of symptoms	−.040	(−0.20)	.278***	(3.35)
Other family member in ill health	.053	(0.06)	1.10***	(2.65)
Local unemployment rate	.135	(1.60)	.098***	(2.89)
Number of observations	212		801	
−2 Log of likelihood functions	112.10		580.22	

Note: Numbers in parentheses are the asymptotic *t*-ratios.
[a]In thousands, 1981 dollars.
***Significant at .01 level.
**Significant at .05 level.
*Significant at .10 level.

symptoms, and local unemployment rate were significant in the decision to stop work for white women but not for nonwhites. Only the weeks worked in 1977 and physical impairment had greater effects for nonwhites. This result may be due in part to the fact that nonwhite families receive a greater share of their income from the wives' earnings than is the case for white families. Also nonwhite women are subject to a greater chance of marital dissolution than white women. If a nonwhite woman realizes her family is more dependent on her income and the chances of her marriage continuing are smaller, she is probably more likely to continue working and to react less to the changes in her family situation, health status, and the local labor market.

Determinants for Whites

Withdrawal rates increase with age. Twelve percent of the white women 45–49 who were employed in 1977 left the labor market by 1982. The withdrawal rate increased to 13.3 percent for the middle age group and 17.6 percent for the oldest third. Because withdrawal rates differed, we decided to see whether the impact of the various factors also varied by age. To this end, the sample was divided into three age groups, and the equations were reestimated.[10] The results are presented in table 6–4.

A mixed picture emerged when we looked at the two prior work variables. Hourly rate of pay had an impact only on the oldest cohort, and weeks worked was more important for the youngest two groups. The smaller impact of prior weeks worked for the 55–59 age group may reflect the fact that some women who formerly had strong work commitment are beginning to retire. On the other hand, a high hourly rate of pay may indicate a better job, which may provide a pension later if the woman continues to work.[11] The number of noncollege dependents and the index of physical impairment had the greatest impact on the oldest group. The level of family income was equally important for the oldest and middle groups; in both cases the effect was considerably greater than that shown for the youngest women. The youngest group is sensitive to changes in husband's income, unlike older women.

In examining the means for the three groups presented in table 6–1, we see that the oldest group is substantially different from the others. Other family income for these women is $5,400 a year less than that of the youngest group. If other family income is available, however, the oldest women will be more likely to take advantage of it and stop working. In a similar fashion, the oldest women have fewer noncollege dependents than the other groups, but when they do have these dependents, this variable has a stronger impact on their continuing to work. On the other hand, this group has a greater degree of physical impairment and is more strongly affected by these physical impairments.

Conclusion

We have attempted to examine some of the reasons women between the ages of 45 and 59 stop working. Starting with women who were employed in 1977, we saw what factors tended to increase and decrease their chance of being employed in 1982. We proposed a rather standard economic model and found that the vast majority of our predictions were confirmed.

In general, there is a strong relationship between a woman's prior commitment to paid employment and her chances of continuing to work. Higher rates of pay did not predict whether white women in their late forties and early fifties will continue to work, but higher pay did decrease the chances of leaving the labor market for nonwhite women and white women in their late fifties. The presence of additional dependents, which causes greater financial

Table 6-4
Logit Analysis of Labor Market Withdrawal of Whites, by Age Group

Independent Variable	Ages 45-49		Ages 50-54		Ages 55-59	
Intercept	-1.87**	(-2.22)	-1.08	(-1.21)	-2.45***	(-3.01)
Hourly rate of pay, 1977	.034	(0.56)	.041	(0.55)	-.173**	(-2.53)
Weeks worked, 1977	-.052***	(-4.47)	-.070***	(-4.96)	-.022*	(-1.68)
Other family income, 1981[a]	.034**	(2.15)	.068***	(3.96)	.068***	(4.82)
Change in husband's income (1976-1981)[a]	.027*	(1.76)	.0005	(0.03)	-.011	(-1.00)
Number of dependent children in college	-.573	(-1.57)	-2.20***	(-2.75)	-.280	(-0.49)
Number of nondependent children in college	-1.61**	(-1.99)	.365	(0.99)	.370	(0.92)
Number of other dependents	-.104	(-0.52)	-.497**	(-1.96)	-1.10***	(2.78)
Index of physical impairment	.082	(1.38)	.132***	(2.70)	.196***	(3.82)
Number of symptoms	.468***	(3.10)	.303**	(2.38)	.297***	(2.74)
Other family member in ill health	1.51**	(2.04)	1.19	(1.37)	1.09*	(1.74)
Local unemployment rate	.105*	(1.77)	.077	(1.25)	.142***	(2.56)
Number of observations	375		348		393	
-2 Log at likelihood function	200.25		194.38		266.29	

Note: Numbers in parentheses are the standard errors of the coefficients.
[a]In thousands, 1981 dollars.
***Significant at .01 level.
**Significant at .05 level.
*Significant at .10 level.

need for a family, also reduced the probability of her stopping work. Higher levels of income from other family members tended to increase the likelihood that she would stop working. Women who reported higher levels of physical incapacity and a greater number of medical symptoms were less likely to remain working, as were women who had other family members suffering from ill health. High local unemployment rates, which increase the likelihood of losing a job and reduce the probabilities of finding a new one, also reduced a woman's chances of continued work.

The results indicate that greater degrees of prior commitment to the labor market increase a woman's chances of staying at work. If her family needs the income from her work, either because of a larger family size or a smaller financial contribution from other family members, this too will keep her working. Health problems will increase her chances of leaving, as will high levels of unemployment.

Notes

1. Our investigation focused on women who reported any work at all during the year prior to the 1977 survey. This includes women who worked year round, as well as women who worked only as a poll worker on election day or perhaps for a few days on a temporary job. We also estimated our model for a group of women who worked twenty-six or more weeks during the year prior to the 1977 survey to exclude those women with only a marginal attachment to the work force. The results were quite similar to those from the sample used in this study. The only major change was a loss of magnitude and statistical significance for the weeks worked coefficient. Another method of choosing the group to study was to include only women who were employed during the survey week in 1977. The model was estimated for this group, and the results were once again quite similar to the ones reported. The major difference was a decline in the magnitude of the weeks worked coefficient.

2. We recognize the large amount of nonmarket work performed by these women. To aid in the exposition of our work, however, the term *work* will refer to market work only.

3. It is impossible to ascertain an actual wage rate for the entire sample in 1982 because 14.5 percent of the group had not worked in the year prior to the survey week. Although a proxy wage rate equation could have been estimated for the group, the 1977 wage rate performed well in the regression equations and was available for the entire set of individuals used in the analysis.

4. The construction of the index is based on the survey respondent's answers to thirteen questions about her ability to perform certain tasks. A 0 was scored if the individual had no difficulty performing the task. A value of 1 was scored if the individual could perform the task but with difficulty and a value of 2 if the task could not be performed at all. The thirteen tasks were walking, using stairs or inclines, standing for long periods of time, sitting for long periods of time, stooping or kneeling, lifting or carrying weights up to ten pounds, lifting or carrying heavy weights, reaching, using

hands and fingers, seeing, hearing, dealing with people, and other activities. Since a value of 0, 1, or 2 could be awarded for each task, the index could take on any value between 0 and 26.

5. This index is constructed by summing up the number of the following symptoms that the woman reported: pain, fainting spells, tiring easily or no energy, weakness or lack of strength, aches or swelling, nervousness or tension, shortness of breath or trouble breathing, and any other symptoms. The index takes on the values of 1 to 8, with the larger values representing a greater number of symptoms.

6. The local unemployment rate used here is the actual local unemployment rate from the CPS. In some cases the woman did not live in a CPS primary sampling unit, and no figure was available for 1982. In order to retain these women from smaller communities in the sample, we imputed a local unemployment rate for them. Figures were available for the local unemployment rate in 1970 for the entire sample. For individuals for whom a 1982 rate was available, we found their 1982 unemployment rate to be on average 1.74 times the 1970 rate. For the individuals whose 1982 rates were not available, we multiplied the 1970 rate by 1.74 to construct the 1982 value.

7. The equations were also run in a weighted ordinary-least-squares form. The difference between the logit and ordinary-least-squares results was negligible.

8. We attempted to determine whether actual loss of a job during the period 1977–1982 led to labor force exit. Women who were fired, laid off, or lost their job through a plant closure may not have been able to secure subsequent employment. An economic displacement binary variable was added to the model to see what effect an involuntary job separation had on leaving the labor market. The coefficient was not statistically significant. Hence the loss of a job did not appear to increase women's chances of stopping work once we controlled for the level of unemployment in the local labor market. However, the reason for leaving a job was not available for all workers, so our lack of results may have been due to the inadequacy of our measure of job loss.

9. We also tried a different form of the model for this group. In place of a measure of the health of other family members, we substituted one that measured the health of the husband. The health of the husband did not have a statistically significant effect on the wife's decision to leave the labor force.

10. The analysis was confined to whites only because once the sample size was divided into age categories, sample sizes for blacks were too small for meaningful analysis.

11. In future research, it would be desirable to test this explanation by including future pension eligibility in the analysis.

7

Factors Affecting Remarriage

Elizabeth Peters

One of the most dramatic and commonly cited consequences of divorce is the decrease in family money income, especially for households headed by divorced women. In 1979 23.1 percent of these households had income below the poverty level compared to 5 percent of married couple families (Current Population Report: Series P-60, no. 130, table A, Series P-23, no. 112, table C). Hoffman (1977), who follows the same families from 1968 to 1974 using the Michigan Panel Survey of Income Dynamics, estimates that income of households headed by women who became divorced during the period fell by 6.7 percent, whereas income of intact husband-wife families rose by 20.8 percent during the same period. Using the NLS, Nestel, Mercier, and Shaw (1983) find that the poverty rate for households headed by women who experienced a divorce (and did not remarry) rose from 10 percent during the survey just prior to divorce to 25 percent during the survey immediately after divorce. Similar results are reported by Mott and Moore (1982) and Espenshade (1979).

Characterizing the economic consequences of divorce can be misleading if one focuses only on the short-term consequences and short-term responses to the loss of earnings of the husband because a large proportion of women who become divorced eventually remarry. This action raises family income considerably. To get a better picture of longer-term consequences, it is necessary to examine the process of transition from divorce to remarriage and the interaction with decisions about employment.

The theoretical framework for analyzing this process will utilize economic search models that have been primarily applied in labor market turnover research and in a few cases have also been applied to marital transitions (see Becker, Landes, and Michael 1977 for the initial development of this idea in the marriage context, and Hutchens 1979 for another application). These models focus on the costs and benefits, both economic and psychological, of finding a new partner and remarrying or remaining single.

The empirical analysis will use proportional hazard models, which estimate rates of transition. Here the hazard models estimate the rates of transition from one state (divorce) to another (remarriage) as a function of exogenous variables. The models allow us to control for the problem of right censoring, which develops when the duration of time to remarriage is not observed for individuals who have not remarried by the most recent observation period. These models allow us to explore the issue of duration dependence (that is, the effect of duration on transition rates). Both features are especially important for the analysis of remarriage. Because remarriage occurs over a period of years, a large number of those who are most recently divorced will have censored durations to remarriage. The inclusion of censored data adds more information because it allows estimation of the entire distribution. The phenomenon of duration dependence is interesting because it may be related to the process of psychological and economic adjustment for women who become divorced.

The sample used for the analysis is women from the NLS mature women's cohort who have been divorced at any time. Divorce and remarriage dates are obtained from a retrospective marital history.

Theoretical Model

Many factors may influence the length of time before remarriage occurs. Higher tastes for marriage and higher costs for finding a spouse will increase the rate of transition into remarriage and reduce the duration of search. Higher income in the single state and fewer opportunities for remarrying will decrease the rate of transition into remarriage and increase the duration of search. Longer durations to remarriage could be viewed negatively because women are spending more time in what is usually a lower income state, but if longer durations reflect a more discriminating search that might lead to a better match, they might also be viewed positively.

A number of variables available from the NLS data can serve as proxies for these theoretical concepts. Family background characteristics such as race, birthplace (foreign, South), and family structure when growing up (intact) may represent tastes for marriage. Characteristics of a woman's marital history at the time of divorce such as number of previous marriages and duration of the previous marriage might be expected to be positively correlated with tastes for marriage and thus with the transition rates to remarriage. The older a woman is at the time of divorce, the fewer are her opportunities for remarriage. After the age of about 30, the ratio of eligible men to women falls as a woman's age increases. Having young children in the household increases the cost of searching for a new spouse, leading to lower transition rates to remarriage. Education can represent both prospects in the divorced state and prospects in the remarried state, so the expected effect of this variable on transition rates is ambiguous.

The impact of employment variables on remarriage rates may work through several different channels. If higher wage potential for a woman is relatively more valuable in the divorced state than in the marriage state (due perhaps to sex role specialization within marriage), then this variable should lower the transition rates to remarriage. In the opposite direction, employment itself may lower the cost of search. Women who stay at home have less opportunity to meet a potential spouse.

Some of these variables have been included in previous studies on remarriage (Becker, Landes, and Michael 1977; Mott and Moore 1982; Nestel, Mercier, and Shaw 1983). Age at divorce is, as predicted, almost always negative and significant. The results for education, children, duration and number of previous marriages, and employment variables have been mixed.

Methodological Issues

Many different statistics can be used to summarize the process of transition from divorce to remarriage. Two of the most intuitively appealing are the mean duration of time to remarriage and the probability of remarriage within a specified time period (for example, within five years of divorce). Problems arise, however, in calculating these statistics when the sample includes recently divorced women. The problem with the first measure is that actual duration of time to remarriage, t, can be observed only for women with completed spells—that is, women who have remarried by the most recent observation period. The distribution of duration time is said to be right censored when durations greater than some value, T, are not observed. One solution for the problem of right censoring is to wait until all the women who ever would remarry have remarried, but this solution has obvious limitations.

Estimating the probability of remarriage within a specified time period, T', circumvents the necessity of observing only completed spells. This procedure requires that all women in the sample be observed at least T' periods between divorce and the last period of observation, and women who do not fit this criterion are excluded from the sample. This procedure throws out information about those who have been most recently divorced. The time period allowed for remarriage is arbitrary, but the larger is T', the more cases that must be excluded from the analysis. Another limitation of this kind of estimation is that it has nothing to say about how the process of transition to remarriage may depend on time itself.

Here we use hazard rate models to estimate rates of transition from one state (divorce) to another (remarriage) as a function of exogenous variables. This technique uses all the information in the sample and can explicitly account for the problem of right censoring or incomplete spells. Another advantage of the technique is that knowledge of the hazard rate is sufficient to calculate the probability of remarriage within a specified time period and the mean duration of time to remarriage.

One of the simplest hazard models assumes that the transition rate from divorce to remarriage is only a function of exogenous variables and not a function of time. That is, the probability that a woman remarries at $t = 1$ given that she is still divorced up to that point is the same as the probability that she remarries at $t = 5$ given that she is still divorced up to that point. It is possible, however, that the hazard rate is not constant over time. Transition rates could decrease with duration, increase with duration, or even increase over some durations and decrease over others.

To illustrate the different results that can be obtained using hazard model estimates versus actual duration values from restricted samples, a data set was created that contains divorced women from the NLS mature women's cohort, and every woman has at least ten years in which to become remarried. Table 7–1 gives the mean duration of time to remarriage for women who were divorced at various ages. Column 1 shows that duration falls as age at divorce increases. This finding contradicts the common belief that older women remarry at a slower rate than do younger women. The discrepancy occurs because the time period between divorce and the last observation date is shorter for women divorced at older ages than for those divorced at younger ages. Therefore those from the former group who remarry by the last observation date will, by sample design, have the shortest durations. Using the second column mitigates this problem somewhat—average duration now increases by age at divorce—but the difference in duration between the youngest and oldest group is still only one year. In column 3 the estimated durations increase dramatically with age at divorce. The difference between columns 2 and 3 for those divorced before age 30 is quite small. As age at

Table 7–1
Comparisons of Mean Duration (in Years) to Remarriage Estimated with Hazard Models and Observed Directly in Restricted Samples

	Mean Duration		Estimated Mean Duration from a Time-Constant Hazard Model[a,b]
Age at Divorce	Only Completed Spells Observed[a]	Includes Censored Observations[a]	
Under 30	4.893	7.533	7.625
30–39	3.728	8.384	12.103
40 and over	3.398	8.569	23.817

[a]Includes only divorced women who have at least ten years in which to remarry before the last observation period.
[b]Estimated duration is $1/\lambda = \exp(X\beta)$.

divorce increases and censored spells become a larger proportion of total spells, however, the difference between columns 2 and 3 becomes much larger.

The Sample

The sample used for the analysis of remarriage rates consists of women from the NLS Mature Women's cohort who have ever been divorced. In 1977 the women gave a retrospective marital history containing information such as the beginning and ending dates of the three most recent marriages, how those marriages ended (for example, divorce or widowhood), and characteristics of the husband in each marriage. This information was updated in the 1982 interview; 1,541 women were eliminated from the analysis because of not being interviewed in 1977 or in 1982. Of the 3,542 women remaining, 927 (26 percent) experienced at least one divorce, and 18.4 percent of these divorced women had two or more divorces by 1982.

To estimate the transition rate to remarriage, both the date of divorce and the date of remarriage (or the date at which a woman was last observed for those who have not remarried) must be available. This restriction further reduced the sample size to 647 observations. In this analysis, each observation represents one divorce event. Women who have experienced more than one divorce may therefore appear several times in the sample.

The ages of the women in 1982 range from 45 to 59. The women in the sample are old enough so that most of the divorces and remarriages after divorce that will ever occur to members of this cohort will already have occurred by 1982. Table 7–2 gives the frequency of age at divorce for women in the sample.

Table 7–2
Distribution of Age at Divorce

Age at Divorce	Frequency	Percentage
14–19	51	7.9
20–24	81	12.5
25–29	97	15.0
30–34	95	14.7
35–39	106	16.4
40–44	97	15.0
45–49	74	11.4
50–54	39	6.0
55–59	7	1.1
Total	647	100.0

The exogenous variables available for this sample include family background characteristics such as birthplace of respondent and respondent's parents, used to control for ethnic and cultural differences, race, and living with both parents when growing up. Variables describing characteristics of the woman at the time of the divorce, such as age at divorce, the presence of children, the length of the former marriage, and number of previous marriages, are also available for the full sample. Means for this sample are given in table 7–3.

In the full sample, 45 percent of the women who were ever divorced were remarried before 1967, the first survey date for the NLS. For these women it is impossible to estimate how economic variables such as labor force partici-

Table 7–3
Means for Full and Restricted Samples

Variable	Full Sample[a]	Restricted Sample[b]
Age at divorce	34.02	39.20
Years married	11.25	14.16
Remarried	.61	.40
Observed duration (in years)[c]	6.92	9.21
More than one divorce	.15	.12
Born 1922–1926	.29	.27
Born 1927–1931	.30	.30
Born 1932 or after	.41	.43
Divorced 1927–1949	.10	.01
Divorced 1950–1959	.26	.10
Divorced 1960–1969	.26	.30
Divorced 1970–1982	.38	.58
White	.74	.74
Intact family at age 14	.66	.66
Foreign parents	.11	.15
Foreign	.02	.03
Education	11.02	11.29
Born South	.14	.12
Any child	.74	.73
Child 05	—	.24
Earnings	—	5843.
In labor force	—	.82
Experience	—	.51
Urban	—	.72
N	618	338

[a]Includes all divorces of members of the NLS mature women's cohort.

[b]Includes only divorces that occurred after the 1967 interview or divorces that occurred before that time if there was no remarriage by the 1967 interview.

[c]Includes censored spells.

pation and wages might influence the transition to remarriage. For this purpose, a second sample is restricted to women who were divorced after 1967 or were divorced before that time but had not remarried as of the first interview date. Means for this sample are shown in table 7–3.

Empirical Results

This section presents estimates of the effects of certain exogenous variables on the transition rates from divorce to remarriage. For the full sample the main focus is on the effect of family background characteristics, demographic characteristics of the women at the time of divorce, and cohort variables. The results in table 7–4 are qualitatively consistent with the findings of several other studies of remarriage that use the probability of remarriage within a given time period as the dependent variable. Whites remarry more quickly than nonwhites. The duration of the previous marriage and the number of previous marriages are also positively related to the transition rate to remarriage. Women who were foreign born or whose parents were foreign born, women with children, and older women take longer to remarry. Growing up in an intact family, being born in the South, and level of education have an insignificant effect on the remarriage rate.

Cohort Effects

It is somewhat surprising to find generally insignificant cohort variable effects both for birth year cohorts (column 1 of table 7–4) and divorce year cohorts (column 2). Differences in remarriage transition rates might have been expected due to changes in the sample of those who become divorced over time or changes in society's attitudes about divorce and remarriage. For example, when divorce was less acceptable and remarriage opportunities were small, women who became divorced were more likely to be the ones for whom the value of the marriage was so low that even the prospect of being divorced for a long time was for them preferable to staying married. As divorce rates increased and remarriage become more commonplace, the possibility of remarriage might have influenced decisions about divorce. Thus expectations about remarriage might increase the likelihood of divorce, and, in turn, those who became divorced would want to remarry more quickly. Differential employment opportunities for each cohort, however, might influence remarriage transition rates in the opposite direction. For example, as labor force participation rates for married women have increased over time, more women have developed the labor market skills needed to support themselves while divorced. This effect could lead to lower remarriage rates

Table 7–4
Transition Rates to Remarriage, Full Sample

Variables	Time-Constant Hazard[a,b]		Time-Dependent Hazard[a,c]
	(1)	(2)	
Constant	−6.92** (23.08)	−6.95** (12.54)	−6.32** (21.66)
White	1.24** (9.02)	1.24** (8.97)	.80** (5.96)
Education	.00 (.17)	.01 (.50)	.01 (.62)
Intact family	.07 (.57)	.08 (.67)	.02 (.22)
Foreign parents	−.51** (2.62)	−.50** (2.55)	−.39** (2.08)
Foreign	−1.07** (2.22)	−1.02** (2.12)	−.30 (.65)
Born South	.06 (.36)	.02 (.15)	−.07 (.44)
Years married	.07** (4.68)	.07** (5.03)	.05** (3.24)
Number of previous marriages	.44** (3.34)	.49** (3.77)	.28** (1.99)
Age at divorce	−.10** (7.79)	−.10** (6.77)	−.10** (7.90)
Any child	−.49** (3.84)	−.48** (3.78)	−.19 (1.53)
Born 1927–1931	.26* (1.87)	—	−.07 (.48)
Born 1932 or after	.12 (0.96)	—	−.30** (2.33)
Divorced 1927–1949	—	.11 (0.36)	—
Divorced 1950–1959	—	.04 (0.17)	—
Divorced 1960–1969	—	0.16 (0.86)	—
t (in years)	—	—	.43** (10.70)
t^2 (in years)	—	—	−.0000908** (11.65)
Max (Log of L)	−3447.69	−3447.97	−3289.38
N	618	618	618

Note: Comprises all divorces that occurred to member of the NLS mature women's cohort.
[a] t-statistics are in parentheses.
[b] $\lambda = \exp(X\beta)$.
[c] $\lambda(t) = \exp(X\beta + \gamma_1 t + \gamma_2 t^2)$
**Denotes significance at .05 level.
*Denotes significance at .10 level.

over time. These counteracting influences are one possible explanation for the apparent stability in remarriage rates across both cohorts. A second possible explanation would be that most of those in the mature women's cohort were born too early to be greatly affected by the dramatic changes in divorce patterns that occurred after the mid- to late 1960s. Adding observations from the young women's cohort might help to determine which of these explanations is correct.

The estimates in table 7–4 can also be used to calculate a different kind of summary measure of the effects of sociodemographic variables on the transition to remarriage: the change in the expected duration, given a change in a given characteristic.[1] Using the numbers in column 1 of table 7–4 and holding other variables constant at the sample mean gives the result that nonwhites have a mean duration to remarriage that is 14.0 years longer than for whites. Having foreign-born parents adds 5.8 years to expected duration, and having children adds 5.5 years to duration. When age at divorce increases by 1 year, expected duration to remarriage increases by 1.2 years, but when the duration of the previous marriage increases by 1 year, expected duration to remarriage falls by 0.7 year. Finally, each additional previous marriage lowers the expected duration to remarriage by 5 years.

Aside from estimating the relationships between exogenous variables and transition rates to remarriage, hazard rate models can also be used to explore the issue of duration dependence, or the way in which transition rates change with duration. If there is no duration dependence, then the conditional probability that a woman will remarry at any point in time is independent of how long she has remained unmarried. Positive duration dependence means that transition rates will increase over time. Such an increase would be consistent with a story where individuals get more proficient in searching for a new spouse as they get more practice. Positive duration dependence can also occur when the reservation value for remarriage falls over time. The initial trauma associated with marital dissolution might cause individuals to require a higher reservation value at first, but that reservation value might fall as the negative associations with the marital breakup recede over time.

Transition rates can also fall with duration. This possibility has two competing explanations: unobserved heterogeneity and negative duration dependence. Heterogeneity occurs when there is an unobserved characteristic, Z, that is positively related to the propensity to remarry, causing those with the highest value of Z to marry first. Average transition rates fall over time because the mean value of Z in the sample that has not yet remarried is falling. Heterogeneity is difficult to distinguish empirically from negative duration dependence. The latter occurs when the experience of being in the divorced state affects the transition rates for a given individual, for example, if there is some stigma attached to remaining unmarried. This effect could compound the negative short-term economic consequences of divorce. On the other hand, if changes over time in tastes for marriage or changes in skills that enhance the value of remaining single are the cause of negative duration dependence, it would indicate that the negative economic consequences of divorce, even for women who do not remarry, are mitigated.

Column 3 in table 7–4 presents the results from a hazard model in which the possibility of duration dependence is introduced.[2] The coefficient estimates on t and t^2 indicate that positive duration dependence dominates over a range of almost 13 years. After that point, the transition rates begin to fall over time, reflecting either heterogeneity in the remaining unmarried population or negative duration dependence.

The introduction of duration dependence into the hazard model causes some changes in the estimates of the parameters of the X variables. The strong positive effect of being white on the transition rate to remarriage is reduced by almost 35 percent. The effects of having foreign parents and a number of previous marriages are also reduced, and the parameter estimates on being foreign born and having any children become insignificant. The coefficients on age at divorce and duration of the previous marriage (years married) appear to be stable across the various models.

Remarriage and Employment

In order to study the effect of labor market variables on the transition to remarriage, it is necessary to restrict the sample to those who were either divorced after the first interview in 1967 or were divorced before 1967 but not remarried by that time. For the first group the variables for earnings, labor force participation, labor market experience, and urban residence are measured as of the survey before divorce. For the second group, these same variables are measured as of the 1967 interview. A variable (separated or divorced) indicating whether the respondent was separated (28.6 percent of the first sample) or divorced (100 percent of the second sample) at the interview when the labor market variables are measured is included in the model. An interaction between this variable and earnings is also included to determine whether women's earnings measured at a time when they are not living with their husbands have a different effect on remarriage transition rates than their earnings at a time when they are still living with their husbands.

The theoretically appropriate variable to measure earnings potential is the expected wage rate at the time of divorce; however, cross-sectional wage regressions for women have notoriously low explanatory power. Because 82 percent of the women in the sample report positive earnings, the confounding effects of the labor force participation decision will be mitigated. Earnings are measured before divorce rather than after because remarriage often leads to a decline in labor force participation (see Mott and Moore 1982). If, instead, earnings after divorce were used to proxy earnings potential, those who remarried the fastest would have lower labor force participation and thus lower observed earnings. This problem would tend to bias the estimated coefficient on earnings downward.

Table 7–5 presents the hazard model results for the restricted sample. The coefficient estimates for the sociodemographic variables are similar to those obtained from the full sample. The dummy variable for white is still strongly positive, and having foreign parents exerts a negative effect on remarriage transition rates. The effects of duration of previous marriage, number of previous marriages, and age at divorce are slightly smaller than in the full sample. This difference could be due to the fact that these characteristics vary less in the restricted sample than in the full sample. Consistent with other research on remarriage probabilities, education becomes negative and significant in the restricted sample.

The negative sign on the earnings variable gives support to the idea of an independent effect. The higher is a woman's earnings potential, the lower are her relative returns to searching for a new spouse. Using the estimates from the time-constant hazard model, an increase in earnings of $1,000 increases mean duration to remarriage by 1.8 years. It is interesting to note, however, that the coefficient estimate on the earnings measured only for those who are not living with their husband is positive, significant, and almost large enough to offset completely the main earnings effect for these women.

One possible explanation for this result is that women without husbands tend to have higher labor force participation rates and tend to work more hours than do women living with their husbands. Therefore higher observed annual earnings for this first group of women might be more a reflection of their hours worked and less a reflection of actual earnings capacity. The positive sign on labor force participation is also consistent with this story. The act of being in the labor force seems to increase the transition rates to remarriage, perhaps because working women have more contact with the pool of potential new partners. Thus search costs are lower. Estimates from the time-constant hazard model show that being in the labor force lowers the mean duration to remarriage by 12.7 years.

The coefficient on the variable indicating the presence of children, which was significant in table 7–4 for the full sample, is insignificant in table 7–5. Having children in the household is highly correlated with labor force participation. In table 7–4 this variable may act only as a proxy for nonparticipation. Thus it would be reasonable for the effect of children to become insignificant when labor force participation is included in the model. The same argument may explain the insignificance of the effect of the labor market experience variable in table 7–5.

In column 2 of table 7–4, the results for the time-dependent hazard model are presented. The parameter estimates for most of the explanatory

Table 7–5
Transition Rates to Remarriage, Restricted Sample

Variables	Time-Constant Hazard[a,b]	Time-Dependent Hazard[a,c]
Constant	−7.98**	−7.10**
	(7.67)	(6.66)
White	1.29**	1.02**
	(4.86)	(3.91)
Education	−.07*	−.06*
	(1.86)	(1.66)
Foreign parents	−.63**	−.61**
	(2.22)	(2.12)
Born South	.53*	.28
	(1.86)	(.96)
Years married	.06**	.05**
	(3.38)	(2.65)
Number of previous marriages	.33*	.26
	(1.83)	(1.38)
Age at divorce	−.05**	−.07**
	(2.09)	(2.81)
Earnings (in $1,000s)	−.08**	−.07**
	(2.25)	(1.97)
Urban	−.13	−0.18
	(.67)	(.91)
In labor force	.56**	.47*
	(2.02)	(1.67)
Sep-Div[d]	−.42	−.42
	(1.34)	(1.34)
SD Earnings (in $1,000s)	.06*	.06
	(1.68)	(1.59)
Divorced 67	−.81**	−.26
	(2.23)	(.73)
Any child	−.24	−.26
	(1.05)	(1.16)
Experience	.06	−.06
	(.16)	(.16)
t (in years)	—	.28**
	—	(4.89)
t^2 (in years)	—	.02**
	—	(5.27)
Max (log of L)	−1329.62	−1307.55
N	338	338

Note: Comprises women divorced after 1967 and women divorced before 1967 who had not remarried by 1967.
[a]t-statistics are in parentheses.
[b]$\lambda = \exp(X\beta)$.
[c]$\lambda(t) = \exp(X\beta + \gamma_1 t + \gamma_2 t^2)$
[d]See appendix 7A.
**Denotes significance at .05 level.
*Denotes significance at .10 level.

variables are remarkably stable. The most striking difference is in the estimate for the dummy variable indicating whether the woman had been divorced before 1967 but not remarried by that time (Div 67). The women still divorced in 1967 have on average very long durations to remarriage; 69 percent of those women have durations of fifteen years or more. Thus in column 1, the negative sign on Div 67 most likely reflects the negative duration dependence captured in the t^2 term in column 2.

All of the hazard models presented thus far have shown very large differences in the remarriage transition rates for whites versus nonwhites. Table 7–6 presents separate hazard model estimates for the two groups. In general the marriage variables—Years Married and Number of Previous Marriages—have more significant and larger effects for nonwhites than for whites. The sociological literature suggests that marriage and divorce are treated much more informally in the black culture. Blacks who have several previous marriages or a long-term previous marriage have indicated an out-of-the-ordinary commitment to the institution of marriage. Therefore it is not surprising to find significantly higher remarriage rates for nonwhites (of whom the larger proportion are blacks) with those characteristics.

For whites the labor market variables have the largest effects. This result makes sense because of the greater variability in labor market behaviors and outcomes among white women than among black women.

Conclusions

Divorce causes economic hardship for many women and their children. Two channels through which these women can improve their situation over time are remarriage and employment. This chapter has explored the transition process from divorce to remarriage as a function of a woman's sociodemographic characteristics and her labor market opportunities.

One of the most striking results is the difference in remarriage rates for whites versus nonwhites. The difference between the two groups in mean duration to remarriage estimated from one model is almost fourteen years. Remarriage rates for nonwhites are more responsive to variables indicating a commitment to the institution of marriage, whereas those for whites are more highly influenced by differences in labor market behavior and employment prospects. White women with higher earnings potential appear to remarry more slowly; however, independent of earnings, women in the labor force remarry more quickly than those not in the labor force. Finally, the hazard models indicate that remarriage transition rates change over time. The transition rates increase over time for a period of thirteen to fifteen years and after that point begin to fall.

Table 7–6
Transition Rates to Remarriage, Restricted Sample, By Race

Variables	Time-Dependent Hazard[a,b] White	Nonwhite
Constant	−6.53** (5.30)	−7.85** (2.23)
Education	−.08* (1.90)	−.05 (.35)
Intact family	.10 (.46)	−.46 (.90)
Foreign parents	−.53* (1.83)	−8.70 (.05)
Born South	.37 (1.04)	−.55 (.67)
Years married	.04** (2.11)	.17** (2.62)
Number of previous marriages	.17 (.81)	1.43* (1.90)
Age at divorce	−.05* (1.80)	−.21** (2.29)
Earnings (in $1,000s)	−.08** (2.15)	−.02 (.12)
Urban	−.20 (.92)	.94 (1.09)
In labor force	.67** (2.13)	.31 (.33)
Sep-Div[c]	−.64* (1.76)	1.12 (.85)
SD Earnings (in $1,000s)	.09** (2.00)	−.02 (.08)
Divorced 67	−.18 (.45)	−.77 (.67)
Any child	−.14 (.54)	−.70 (.94)
Experience	.09 (.19)	−.72 (.70)
t (in years)	−.23** (3.32)	.69** (5.36)
t^2 (in years)	.02** (3.98)	.03** (4.99)
Max (log of L)	−1081.95	−201.27
N	250	87

Note: Comprises women divorced after 1967 and women divorced before 1967 who had not remarried by 1967.
[a]t-statistics are in parentheses.
[b]$\lambda(t) = \exp(X\beta + \gamma_1 t + \gamma_2 t^2)$
[c]See appendix 7A.
**Denotes significance at .05 level.
*Denotes significance at .10 level.

Appendix 7A

Table 7A–1
Variable Definitions

Variable	Definition
Years married	Duration in years of previous marriage
Remarried	Dummy variable equal to 1 if respondent remarried by 1982 survey
Duration (*t*)	Duration in years of time between divorce and remarriage (or 1982 survey date for censored observations)
Born 1922–1926 Born 1927–1931 Born 1932 or after	Dummy variable equal to 1 if respondent was born during specified interval
Divorced 1927–1949 Divorced 1950–1959 Divorced 1960–1969 Divorced 1970–1982	Dummy variable equal to 1 if respondent was divorced during specified interval
White	Dummy variable equal to 1 if respondent's race is white
Intact	Dummy variable equal to 1 if respondent lived with both parents when she was fourteen years old
Foreign parents	Dummy variable equal to 1 if either of respondent's parents were born outside the United States or Canada
Foreign	Dummy variable equal to 1 if respondent was born outside the United States or Canada
Education	Number of years of education completed by respondent by 1967
Born South	Dummy variable equal to 1 if respondent was born in the South
Any child	Dummy variable equal to 1 if respondent had any children younger than 18 at time of divorce
Child 05[a]	Number of children less than 6 years old living in respondent's household the survey before divorce
Earnings[a]	Respondent's wage and salary earnings reported the survey before divorce. Earnings are equal to 0 if respondent did not report any earnings
In labor force[a]	Dummy variable equal to 1 if respondent reported any earnings the survey before divorce
Experience[a]	Proportion of years respondent worked six months or more between leaving school and the survey before divorce
Urban[a]	Dummy variable equal to 1 if respondent lived in urban area the survey before divorce
Sep-Div[a]	Dummy variable equal to 1 if the woman was not living with her husband the survey before divorce
SD Earnings	Interaction between earnings and sep-div
Div 67	Dummy variable equal to 1 if respondent was divorced before 1967 survey but not remarried by that time; equal to 0 if respondent became divorced after 1967 survey

[a]When Div 67 = 1, these variables are measured as of the 1967 interview.

Notes

1. This measure is calculated as

$$\frac{\partial E(t)}{\partial X} = -\frac{\alpha}{\lambda}$$

where α is the parameter estimate reported for characteristic X in column 1 of table 7-4.

2. The form of the hazard rate, $\lambda = \exp(X\beta + \lambda_1 t + \lambda_2 t^2)$, allows for positive duration dependence, negative duration dependence, or both.

References

Becker, G.S.; Landes, E.M.; and Michael, R.T. 1977. "An Economics Analysis of Marital Instability." *Journal of Political Economy* 85, no. 6.

Espenshade, T.J. 1979. "The Economics Consequences of Divorce." *Journal of Marriage and the Family* 41, no. 3 (August).

Hoffman, S. 1977. "Marital Instability and the Economic Status of Women." *Demography* 14, no. 1 (February).

Hutchens, R.M. 1979. "Welfare, Remarriage, and Marital Search." *American Economic Review* 69, no. 3 (June).

Menken, J.; Trussel, J.; Stempel, D.; and Babakof, O. 1981. "Proportional Hazards Life Table Models: An Illustrative Analysis of Socio-Demographic Influences on Marriage Dissolution in the United States." *Demography* 18, no. 2 (May).

Mott, F.L., and Moore, S.F. 1982. "Marital Transitions and Employment." In F.L. Mott, ed., *The Employment Revolution*. Cambridge: MIT Press.

———. 1983. "The Tempo of Remarriage among Young American Women." *Journal of Marriage and the Family* (May).

Nestel, G.; Mercier, J.; and Shaw, L.B. 1983. "Economic Consequences of Midlife Change in Marital Status." In L.B. Shaw, ed., *Unplanned Careers: The Working Lives of Middle-Aged Women*. Lexington, Mass.: Lexington Books.

Ross, H.L., and Sawhill, I.V. 1975. *Time of Transition*. Washington, D.C.: Urban Institute.

Tuma, N.B.; Hannan, M.T.; and Groeneveld, L.P. 1979. "Dynamic Analysis of Event Histories." *American Journal of Sociology* 84:820–854.

8
Looking toward Retirement: Plans and Prospects

Lois B. Shaw

By 1982 a few women in the NLS mature women's sample had already retired; over the next twenty years virtually all will retire. This chapter looks at the retirement plans and economic prospects for this cohort of women. At present the elderly population as a whole has a poverty rate of about 14 percent, one percentage point below that of the population as a whole. Within the elderly population, however, women are at greater risk of poverty than men; among those aged 65 and over, 17 percent of women and only 10 percent of men are poor (U.S. Bureau of the Census 1985a, table 21). The risk of poverty for elderly women is strongly related to marital status and race. Only 6 percent of white married women are poor, as compared with 19 percent of black married women. Among unmarried women, 20 percent of white women, and nearly half of black women aged 65 and over are poor. Just under 40 percent of white women and only one-quarter of black women are married at this age.

Women who are now approaching retirement age are more likely to have worked long enough to be eligible for a pension than their counterparts among older women. In addition, changes in pension laws may make it more likely that women will receive pension benefits from their own work or from survivor benefits available through their husbands' pensions.

The first part of this chapter examines expectations for receiving pensions among women in the NLS sample and makes comparisons with pension receipt by older women. Expected receipt of Social Security benefits and the extent of reliance on Social Security are also examined. The second part describes the retirement plans of women in the NLS sample and analyzes the determinants of their planned age of retirement.

Economic Prospects for the Retirement Years

In 1982 only 20 percent of women aged 65 and over reported that they received any income from pensions other than Social Security (U.S. Bureau of

Scott Martin provided excellent research assistance for this chapter.

Table 8–1

Pension Eligibility of Women Aged 45–59 in 1982, By Race and Marital Status

(percentage)

	Black		White		
	Married	*Unmarried*	*Married*	*Unmarried*	*Total*
Already receiving pension	2.2	0.3	1.3	1.5	1.3
Vested[a]	18.8	17.7	18.0	24.8	19.5
Expect to become eligible	5.5	12.0	9.2	19.3	11.2
Don't know whether will stay	2.2	1.9	1.7	1.9	1.8
Don't plan to stay	0.6	2.9	2.1	1.4	1.9
No pension with current or past employer	24.7	18.3	16.8	18.1	17.5
Not employed or self-employed, no pension from previous job	44.9	42.0	49.7	31.7	45.3
Don't know	1.1	4.8	1.4	1.2	1.5
Total	100.0	100.0	100.0	100.0	100.0
N	472	476	1,942	597	3,487

[a]Eligible to receive a pension later if left job today or eligible for a pension from a previous job.

the Census 1985b, table 50). It appears that women who are now approaching retirement age will be considerably more likely to have pensions than are women now past retirement age. As table 8–1 shows, 32 percent of the entire NLS women's cohort have or expect to have pensions of their own when they retire; another 2 percent are working for companies with pension plans but are uncertain whether they will stay long enough to become eligible. These figures are for all women in the sample, including those who were not employed in 1982. Even if some of the women who now expect to work long enough to receive pensions are disappointed in their plans, it seems probable that the receipt of pensions by elderly women will increase in the future.

Unmarried women are more likely to expect to have pensions than their married counterparts. Forty-five percent of unmarried white women expect to have pensions as compared with only 28 percent of married women. The differences between black unmarried and married women are much smaller; 30 percent of unmarried women expect pensions compared with 26 percent of married women. Differences between blacks and whites are much greater for unmarried than for married women.

After retirement some women will have access to pensions earned by their husbands. In the past many women did not receive survivor benefits after they became widowed. Although the Employee Retirement Income Security Act (ERISA) has since 1974 required that employers with pension plans offer joint and survivor options, apparently many men did not elect these options. In addition, some plans made no provision for survivor benefits if the husband died before reaching retirement age. The passage of PL 98-397 in 1984 requires that survivors' benefits be automatic unless they have been waived in writing by both spouses. In addition, the law protects survivor benefits from forfeiture in the case of a vested worker who dies before retirement. To illustrate the potential importance of this change, about 30 percent of widows in the NLS who were aged 55–59 in 1982 reported that they were receiving or would receive survivor benefits from their husbands' pensions. In contrast, nearly 60 percent of married women of the same age reported that their husbands were receiving or expected to receive pensions. Although some of this difference was undoubtedly due to greater mortality among men who had held jobs that would not have carried a pension in any event, part of the difference was probably due to the husband's failure to elect a survivor benefit option or to pension plans that offered no survivor benefits if the employee died before reaching retirement age. Most of the NLS women currently married to men with pensions should receive benefits from those pensions in the future, either as spouses or survivors. About 70 percent of these women do not expect to have pensions of their own, so this law is potentially important for the retirement security of many of them.

Table 8–2 shows the distribution of expected pensions from their own and their husbands' jobs for the entire sample by race and marital status. For the unmarried women, it is assumed that only widows have pensions from their husbands since up to the present, divorce settlements have seldom included any participation in the spouse's pension. The majority of black unmarried women will probably have no pension other than Social Security, but slightly over half of unmarried white women will probably have their own pension or survivor benefits from their husbands. Nearly 60 percent of black married women and over 70 percent of white married women should have access to pensions; about 20 percent of married women of both races expect to have pensions from both spouses.

Overall about 65 percent of all women who are now 45–59 years of age expect to have pensions when they retire—either from their own employment or from their husbands'. If these expectations are realized, this new generation of retired women should be considerably better off than are women currently age 65 and over. At present probably about 40 percent of women aged 65 and over have access to pensions from their own or their husbands' employment.[1]

It is possible that actual pension receipt is being considerably overestimated by women in the NLS. Some of these women may lose pensions because

Table 8–2
Eligibility of Families for Respondent's or Husband's Pension, by Race and Marital Status
(percentage)

	Black			White		
	Married	*Unmarried*	*Total*	*Married*	*Unmarried*	*Total*
Respondent's pension only	8.1	28.2	18.0	7.9	41.0	15.6
Husband's pension only	30.3	6.6	18.8	42.2	6.9	33.8
Both have pensions	18.2	1.8	10.2	20.5	4.5	16.8
Neither	29.8	53.1	41.1	22.6	42.2	27.1
Don't know[a]	13.4	10.3	12.0	6.8	5.2	6.6
Total	100.0	100.0	100.0	100.0	100.0	100.0
N	472	476	948	1,942	597	2,539

[a]Including don't know whether the respondent will stay on her job long enough to receive a pension.

they or their husbands lose their jobs or become ill or because they lose access to husbands' pensions through divorce. In addition, a study of recent retirees by the Social Security Administration found that approximately 20 percent of retirees with private pensions had elected to take lump sum benefits instead of pensions (Iams 1985). For all of these reasons, actual pension receipt may be considerably less than the NLS figures suggest. Nevertheless, these data do suggest that the economic position of elderly women should improve in the future as the result of women's longer work histories and changes in the law regarding survivor benefits.

For older black women, conditions appear much less favorable: fewer than half expect to receive pensions. These figures reflect the lower levels of pension eligibility among black men and unmarried black women and the fact that far fewer black women than white women are currently married.

In spite of the increasing access to private pensions among this generation of women, Social Security remains an important part of their anticipated retirement income. Over 90 percent of the sample report that they expect to be eligible for Social Security either on their own or their husband's account. When asked to name the three most important sources of income, over 85 percent mentioned Social Security as an important source of income when they retire. Just under half of the sample anticipate that Social Security will be their most important source of income.

As table 8–3 shows, anticipated dependence on Social Security in retirement varies considerably among different groups of women. Over 60 percent

Table 8–3
Most Important Source of Income in Retirement, Women Aged 45–59 in
1982, by Race and Marital Status
(percentage)

	Black			White		
	Married	*Unmarried*	*Total*	*Married*	*Unmarried*	*Total*
Social Security	64.3	62.7	63.5	44.4	56.8	47.3
Pension	25.4	16.6	21.0	38.8	22.3	34.9
Income from assets	0.2	0.4	0.3	8.3	7.7	8.2
Other[a]	2.4	7.8	5.1	4.2	7.1	4.9
No source mentioned	7.7	12.5	10.1	4.3	6.1	4.7
Total	100.0	100.0	100.0	100.0	100.0	100.0
N	477	482	959	1,976	607	2,583

[a]Includes earnings, Supplementary Security Income, welfare, and disability income.

of black women, whether currently married or not, expect that Social Security will be their most important source of retirement income. Fifty-seven percent of unmarried white women also name Social Security as their most important income source. Only among white married couples does the percentage counting on Social Security as their most important source of income fall below 50 percent.

Nearly 40 percent of white married women mentioned pensions other than Social Security as their most important source of retirement income. For this group other pensions approach Social Security in importance. This is far from the case for the other groups: only one-quarter of black married women mentioned pension income as most important, and even smaller numbers of unmarried women of either race listed pension income first.

About 8 percent of white women expect income from interest, dividends, and other assets to be their most important source of income in retirement; the percentage of black women expecting asset income to be most important is close to zero. About 7 percent of unmarried women of both races list other sources of income as most important; these sources include earnings, Supplementary Security Income, and other welfare income. About 10 percent of black women do not know what source of income will be important or do not list any source.

Determinants of Retirement Plans

Research using the Social Security Retirement History Survey has found that the employment of wives of the men in that sample was influenced by their husbands' retirement decisions but that the wives' own earnings potential and pension eligibility were important as well (Clark, Johnson, and McDermed 1980; Anderson, Johnson, and McDermed 1980; Henretta and O'Rand 1980). Furthermore, other research suggests that wives' continued employment also increases the probability that husbands will continue to work as the couple approaches or passes the usual retirement age (Hall and Johnson 1980; Clark, Johnson, and McDermed 1980; Morgan 1980). In addition, characteristics of both spouses, including their respective wages and pensions, have been found to influence the probability of joint retirement as opposed to one spouse's retiring before the other (Henretta and O'Rand 1983). In a study using the NLS older men's sample, husbands' pension eligibility was found to increase the likelihood that wives would retire; wives' pension eligibility also increased the likelihood that husbands would retire before age 62 but not at later ages (Shaw and Gagen 1984). For unmarried women, health and potential income after retirement have been shown to be major influences on the timing of retirement (O'Rand and Henretta 1982).

An earlier analysis of married women's retirement plans, using questions asked of the NLS mature women's sample in 1979, found that women's pension eligibility and their husbands' retirement plans were the principal influences on women's retirement plans (Shaw 1984). The present report extends this earlier analysis in several ways. First, assuming that husbands' plans are a determinant of wives' plans, as the earlier analysis did, implies that the husbands' plans are made independently and the wives' plans are contingent on husbands' plans. Evidence of joint determination of plans makes it more desirable to include the determinants of husbands' plans—pension eligibility and health—directly in the analysis. Second, a more extensive set of questions in the 1982 interview makes possible rough estimates of pension size effects on women's retirement. Third, both married and unmarried women's plans are included in the analysis. Finally, quality of employment variables are added to the analysis. Although financial considerations are probably the most important determinants of retirement, workers may be less motivated to retire early from jobs that are interesting and satisfying. Whether workers nearing retirement age can be persuaded to retire later by redesigning the content of their jobs may become an important question as the size of the elderly population increases.

The first part of the analysis focuses on the entire sample of women who responded to the question on planned age of retirement in 1982. Separate analyses of the determinants of early retirement (before age 62) and average retirement (before age 65) are presented by race and by marital status. In these equations, variables for pension eligibility are included, but no attempt is made to measure pension size. Women who do not know when they will retire are excluded from the analysis; women who say they plan never to retire are included with the 65 and over group.

In the second part of the analysis, estimates are made of the effects of pension amount for the white sample aged 55–59. The reason for this age limitation is that pension amount often depends on maximum earnings or earnings in the final years of employment. If women who are still in their forties are included, present earnings are likely to be considerably below their maximum. Rather than attempting to adjust earnings for age in estimating pension amount, I have chosen to use a narrow age range of women, close to the end of their employment, to estimate the effect of pension amount on retirement plans. The basic equations to be estimated are as follows:

Whether plan to retire before age x $= f$(PENSION, ASSETS, HEALTH, SATIS, HUSHEALTH, HUSPENSION).

The equations for the entire sample contain a series of pension dummies indicating whether the respondent is eligible to receive a pension before age x, ELINOW; at a later age, ELILATE; or at some time but age unknown, DKA; no pension is the omitted category.[2] Since self-employed women were not asked the questions on current pension, SELF is included as another dummy variable indicating that the woman's current job falls into this category. The expectation is that women will be more likely to plan to retire once they become eligible for a pension and will postpone retirement if they will become eligible later. Self-employed women are expected to plan for later retirement than other women, in part because the self-employed can more easily reduce their hours and work effort without actually retiring.

The equations for the 55–59 age sample make use of questions on the number of years of experience with the current employer and current earnings. Although pension plans vary greatly in their rules for computing benefits, most pensions are related to length of service and level of earnings. The proxy for the size of the pension before age x, PENAMT = earnings times length of service times ELINOW. Length of service is the current number of years the respondent has worked for her employer plus the additional number of years she would work if she were to continue until age 60 (for $x = 62$) or age 62 (for $x = 65$). A second variable, ADDBEN, measures the maximum additional amount that would be gained by waiting to age x or to any time up to age 70. For women who were not eligible before age x but would be eligible later, ADDBEN is a large positive amount. For women who were already eligible before age x, present values of future benefit amounts were calculated, and ADDBEN was the difference between PENAMT and the largest future amount; this value could be positive or negative.[3]

Plans for retirement are probably affected not only by the amount of pension available at a given age and the added amount that would become available at a later date but also by the amount that the woman could earn if she continued to work. As a proxy for this amount, EARN82, the amount of the respondent's earnings in 1982 is included in the equations that contain estimated benefit amounts. It is expected that the higher a woman's earnings, the less likely she is to plan to retire.

Because of a high rate of missing information on assets, the ASSETS variable used is a dummy variable "asset income important" taken from questions on expected sources of income in retirement. If asset income is important, the respondent will probably be financially more able to consider early retirement. The relationship of ASSETS and retirement plans is therefore expected to be positive. Variables reflecting eligibility for Social Security were included in preliminary analyses; these proved not to be significant, perhaps due to collinearity with other variables or almost universal eligibility at given ages.

Women with more health problems are expected to plan to retire early. The measure of health problems is HEALTH, the sum of the number of functional limitations and symptoms reported by the respondent.[4]

Several measures of job satisfaction were investigated. The one used in the equations reported here is LIKE, which measures satisfaction with intrinsic features of the job. LIKE is a scale based on questions about factors liked most about the current job. Each mention of an intrinsic feature is scored as 1; the scale can take any values from 0 through 3. Alternative job satisfaction measures that were used will be described later.

Variables expected to affect a married woman include the major influences on her husband's retirement: his health and his eligibility for a pension. The effect of the husband's health on his wife's retirement plans is uncertain. If the husband's health forces him to retire early, the wife may feel the need to work longer to meet the family's financial needs. But for some kinds of illness or disability, she might be needed at home to provide personal care for him. HUSHEALTH is a dummy variable taking the value of 1 if the husband is reported as having a health problem that limits the amount or kind of work he can do.

A series of pension variables are also included for the husband. A difficulty here is that his age of pension eligibility was not asked, so except for husbands already receiving pensions, the age of first eligibility is unknown. The variables used essentially interact husband's pension eligibility with his age. HUSHAS takes a value of 1 if the husband is covered by a pension plan and will be 65 before the wife reaches age x or if he is already receiving a pension. HUSMAY takes a value of 1 if the husband is covered by a pension and will be aged 62–64 before the wife reaches age x, and HUSLATE takes a value of 1 if the husband is covered by a pension but will not be 62 before the wife reaches age x. When married and unmarried women are included in the same equation, NMAR is added to indicate that the respondent is not married. In this case, the married woman whose husband has no pension can be considered the omitted category for the combined series of HUSPENSION and NMAR variables. If the husband is already receiving or is eligible to receive a pension by the time the wife reaches age *x*, she may be more likely to plan to retire. If he is not yet eligible, the effect of his having a pension in the future is not certain. If the pension is thought of as an asset, the wife may feel less constrained to continue working, but if the couple prefers to retire at the same time, she may plan to wait until her husband can begin actually receiving a pension. Women who are not married will generally have fewer financial resources than married women and are expected to plan to retire at a later age than their married counterparts.

Results

Table 8–4 shows the reported plans for retirement by women who were working or planning to return to work as of the 1982 interview date. Generally married women plan to retire before unmarried women; black married women are less likely to plan to retire before age 60 but more likely to plan to retire at age 62. Black women are more likely to respond that they do not know when they will stop working. The prevalence of plans to retire at ages 62 and 65, points when Social Security and many pension plans begin, is clearly shown. Similar but smaller bunching of retirement plans at ages 55 and 60 are apparent from a year-by-year breakdown of the data.

Table 8–5 shows the regression equations for the determinants of planning to retire before age 62 for the total white and black samples and married

Table 8–4
Women's Planned Retirement Age in 1982, by Marital Status and Race
(percentage)

| Planned Retirement Age | Black | | White | | |
	Married	Unmarried	Married	Unmarried	Total
Already	0.6	0.5	0	0.3	0.4
Less than 55	1.8	3.4	0.7	0.5	2.4
55–59	10.3	11.08	7.5	6.1	10.1
60–61	8.3	10.0	4.7	5.5	8.6
62	21.8	19.3	18.8	20.7	19.8
63–64	0.6	0.9	0	0.9	0.9
65	14.1	17.8	21.2	25.3	19.6
More than 65	1.2	1.8	2.4	3.0	2.1
Never	7.4	7.6	10.9	13.0	9.0
Don't know	33.9	26.8	33.8	24.9	27.2
Total	100.0	100.0	100.0	100.0	100.0
N	299	1,209	321	462	2,298

Table 8–5
Regression Equations for Determinants of Planning to Retire before Age 62, by Race and Marital Status

	Black			White		
	Total	*Married*	*Unmarried*	*Total*	*Married*	*Unmarried*
ELINOW	.369***	.379***	.343***	.261***	.270***	.234***
ELILATE	-.057	-.120	-.009	-.107***	-.098**	-.136***
DKA	.082	.193	-.011	.079'	.110*	.004
SELF	-.025	.152	-.107	-.105	-.098	-.135
ASSETS	.094	.011	.156*	.029	.027	.036
HEALTH	-.000	-.001	-.000	-.001	-.002	.002
LIKE	.032	.082*	-.004	-.018	-.010	-.033
HUSHEALTH	-.026	-.021	a	-.077***	-.076*	a
HUSHAS	.084	.090	a	.038	.037	a
HUSMAY	.093	.103	a	.107**	.103*	a
HUSLATE	.248*	.254*	a	.022	.020	a
NMAR	-.090	a	a	-.176***	a	a
Constant	.174**	.129*	.113	.307***	.295***	.162***
R̄²	.159	.145	.129	.134	.088	.132
N	342	167	175	1,048	738	310

aNot used in this equation.
***Significant at .01 level.
**Significant at .05 level.
*Significant at .10 level.

and unmarried women of each race. Means of the variables used in the analysis are shown in table 8A–1.

The most important predictor of plans for early retirement for all groups is being eligible for a pension before age 62. White women in all categories are less likely to plan to retire before age 62 if they will become eligible for a pension at a later date, but this variable is not significant for black women. Black unmarried women who expect asset income to be important are more likely to plan to retire early, but this variable has no effect for other groups.[5]

The respondent's health does not affect her plans for early retirement. This result, also found in the analysis of the 1979 data (Shaw 1984), is probably due to the fact that women with severe health problems have already left the labor force and are therefore excluded from the sample.

Satisfaction with intrinsic features of the job does not enter into plans for early retirement for any group; in fact black married women who score high on the intrinsic satisfaction scale are more likely to plan to retire early. When a general job satisfaction measure was substituted for the intrinsic features scale, this new measure also failed to show any influence on plans for early retirement for most groups. The exception was black married women, but in this case high satisfaction had a negative and marginally significant influence on retirement plans. Regarding plans for early retirement, it appears that the intrinsic interest of the job is not important for any group, nor is general job satisfaction very important.

Having a husband with health limitations decreases the probability of planning to retire early for white women but not for blacks. In chapter 5 we saw that husband's disability tended to decrease the wife's hours worked. This difference in results may be due to the fact that women who responded to their husband's health problems by leaving the labor force are excluded from the retirement plans sample, leaving only women who are responding to income loss or anticipated loss by planning to work longer.

The husband's pension variables are only sporadically significant, and the variable that might be expected to have the biggest impact, HUSHAS (denoting that the husband is already eligible), is not significant for either blacks or whites. A combined pension variable that does not take husband's age into account (not shown) was significant for blacks but not whites. The pension variables could fail to perform as expected because we do not know whether the husbands will be eligible for pensions at a given time or because husbands' pensions are not a very important factor in wives' plans for retiring at an early age.

Table 8–6 shows the equations for planning to retire before age 65 for these same race and marital status groups. Being eligible for their own pensions is again a significant determinant of retirement plans for all groups; being eligible later defers plans for retirement for white women as before but now attains significance for married black women as well. White married

Table 8–6
Regression Equations for Determinants of Planning to Retire before Age 65, by Race and Marital Status

	Black			White		
	Total	Married	Unmarried	Total	Married	Unmarried
ELINOW	.316**	.384**	.260**	.211**	.170**	.318**
ELILATE	-.089	-.084	-.237	-.226**	-.211**	-.211*
DKA	.110	.304*	-.048	.014	.017	.028
SELF	-.154	-.127	-.134	-.243**	-.266**	-.129
ASSETS	-.012	-.087	.052	.022	.029	-.005
HEALTH	-.001	.000	-.008	.004	-.000	.014*
LIKE	-.036	-.028	-.051	-.041*	-.035	-.057*
HUSHEALTH	-.021	-.016	—	-.006	-.000	—
HUSHAS	.060	.026	—	.084*	.088*	—
HUSMAY	.163	.108	—	-.006	-.000	—
NMAR	-.129*	—	—	-.162**	—	—
Constant	.545**	.500**	.484**	.572**	.582**	.363**
$\bar{R}^2$	.101	.104	.063	.123	.078	.139
N	342	167	175	1,048	738	310

**Significant at .05 level.
*Significant at .10 level.

women who are self-employed are also less likely to plan to retire before age 65. Assets are not important for any group.

Although health status did not affect plans for retiring before age 62, white unmarried women's plans for retiring before age 65 are influenced by their health. In a study of the influences on retirement plans of older men, Parnes and Nestel (1974) found that men with health limitations were more likely to plan to retire before age 65. We find a similar result for unmarried women but not for married women. Probably married women with health problems that would be severe enough to affect retirement plans are more likely to be financially able to leave the labor force and are thus already excluded from our sample. Unmarried women are more likely to continue to work even if they have health problems. These problems do not appear to increase the chances that they will plan to retire before age 62, but after this age, with Social Security benefits and other pensions available, health is more likely to be a consideration in their plans.

Although it had no effect at an earlier age, satisfaction with intrinsic features of the job significantly decreases the chances of retiring before age 65 for white women, and unmarried women are those most affected. This result may indicate that employment is an important source of interest and life satisfaction for some women who do not have the alternative role of housewife to resume when they retire.

That intrinsic job satisfaction is not a significant factor for black women may be due to the fact that so few hold jobs that are interesting and fulfilling. When another scale measuring dissatisfaction with the job because it was difficult, dangerous, or demanding was added to the equations (results not shown), black women and unmarried white women with a high score on this variable were significantly more likely to plan to retire before age 65. These results suggest that for some groups, both positive and negative aspects of their jobs influence their retirement plans. These factors, as well as economic incentives, may need to be considered if society wants to encourage later retirement in the future.

Husband's health, a deterrent to plans for early retirement for white women, does not have an impact on whether women plan to retire before or after age 65; however, husbands' pensions now become a significant influence on white wives' retirement plans, particularly if the husband already has a pension before the wife reaches age 65. For black women, husbands' pensions are not a signficiant influence.

In order to determine whether pension amounts as well as eligibility affect retirement plans, we turn to an analysis of the retirement plans of women who were aged 55–59 in 1982. Because of small sample sizes, black women's plans were not analyzed, nor could an analysis by marital status be performed for white women. Table 8–7 shows the results of two analyses: equation 1 is the same as the equations previously reported for the entire

Table 8–7
Regression Equations: Determinants of Planned Age of Retirement, White Women, Age 55–59

	Retire before 62		Retire before 65	
	(1)	(2)	(1)	(2)
EARN82	a	−.002	a	−.006
ELINOW	.238***	a	.289***	a
ELILATE	−.055	a	−.135	a
PENAMT	a	.054***	a	.066***
ADDBEN	a	−.005	a	−.054
DKA	.057	.061	.013	−.012
SELF	.042	.046	−.267**	−.291**
ASSETS	.023	.038	−.005	−.015
HEALTH	.006	.006	.005	.007
LIKE	−.048*	−.057**	−.046	−.056*
HUSHEALTH	−.015	−.004	.049	.044
HUSHAS	.092	.100	.151**	.176**
HUSMAY	.007	.008	.040	.059
HUSLATE	.066	.087	a	a
NMAR	−.121**	−.108*	−.203***	−.172**
Constant	.180***	.188***	.540***	.632***
$\bar{R}^2$	.096	.102	.176	.166
N	312	312	312	312

a Variable not included in this equation.
***Significant at .01 level.
**Significant at .05 level.
*Significant at .10 level.

sample, while equation 2 substitutes the proxy variables for pension amount now (PENAMT) and the added amount from waiting to retire (ADDBEN) for ELINOW and ELILATE. Amount of respondent's earnings (EARN82) is also added to equation 2. Means of all variables are shown in table 8A–2.

The variable for current pension amount is significant, but the variable for additional benefits through waiting is not. These results parallel those for the eligibility variables. Each $100,000 in pension amount increases the probability of retiring before age 62 by 5 percentage points and before age 65 by 7 percentage points. Recalling that pension amount is the product of current earnings and length of time the respondent will have worked for her employer if she stays until she is age 60 (for $x = 62$) or age 62 (for $x = 65$), we might attempt to convert pension amount into actual pension size. For example, in a rather generous pension plan such as that for the state of Ohio, each $100,000 of pension amount would yield approximately $2,000 per year in pension benefits at age 65 and slightly less at younger ages. For such a pension plan each $1,000 in pension benefits would increase the probability of planning to retire early by about 3 percentage points. Many pensions, however, are much less generous, and the overall effect of a $1,000 increase in actual benefits is probably considerably greater than this estimate. The coefficient on the earnings variable is negative, as expected, but not statistically significant.

Comparing table 8–7 with tables 8–5 and 8–6 reveals several minor differences between the aged 55–59 sample and the entire sample. One difference is that intrinsic interest of the job becomes a significant factor in early retirement plans for the older group of women who are closer to the actual retirement decision. Becoming eligible for a pension at a later date is less of a deterrent, as is husband's health.

One problem with analyzing the aged 55–59 group is that some women in this group had already stopped working by 1982, and the sample is therefore truncated. In fact, when women who were working in 1979 but had stopped working by 1982 and did not plan to return to work were included in the retired sample, some interesting differences appear (table 8–8). Current pensions become less significant and future eligibility more so. Husband's health again becomes a deterrent to early retirement. In addition, the respondent's own health becomes significant, indicating that actual retirement, as opposed to plans, may be influenced by unanticipated health problems.

Summary

Nearly one-third of all women now approaching retirement age expect to have pensions of their own when they retire; about 65 percent expect that they will receive pension income from their own jobs or as spouses or survivors of husbands with pensions. These figures compare favorably with the 20 percent of women age 65 and over who now receive pensions as individuals and the 40 percent who live in families in which they or their husbands receive pensions. Economic prospects for the retirement years are less promising for black women: less than half expect to have pensions from any source, and only 37 percent of black women who are not currently married expect to have pensions in the future. Black women, and unmarried white women as well, will therefore be heavily dependent on Social Security income when they reach the retirement years. About 45 percent of white married women also expect that Social Security will be their most important source of retirement income.

The retirement plans of middle-aged working women are strongly influ-

Table 8–8
Regression Equations for Planned Age of Retirement Including Women Who Retired between 1979 and 1982: White Women, Aged 55–59

	Retire before 62	Retire before 65
ELINOW	.068	.204***
ELILATE	– .249***	– .234***
DKA	.030	.002
SELF	– .083	– .321***
ASSETS	.048	.019
HEALTH	.029***	.019***
LIKE	– .057**	– .038
HUSHEALTH	– .097*	– .019
HUSHAS	.106*	.106*
HUSMAY	.023	.002
HUSLATE	.008	a
NMAR	– .177***	– .213***
Constant	.366***	.626
$\bar{R}^2$	.182	.159
N	437	437

^aNot used in this equation.

***Significant at the .01 level.

**Significant at the .05 level.

*Significant at the .10 level.

enced by their eligibility for pensions and the amount of pension they may receive. Husband's pensions are less important, at least in the plans women are currently making. These women tend to plan to postpone retirement if their husbands have a health problem. Some women, especially those who are not married, may plan to retire later if they find their work intrinsically interesting and satisfying.

Appendix 8A

Table 8A–1
Means of Variables Used in Regression Analyses

	Black			White		
	Total	Married	Unmarried	Total	Married	Unmarried
ELINOW						
$X = 62$	.213	.216	.211	.249	.243	.265
$X = 65$	.345	.329	.360	.411	.392	.458
ELILATE						
$X = 62$	.181	.162	.200	.236	.207	.303
$X = 65$	.047	.042	.051	.073	.058	.110
DKA	.120	.102	.137	.100	.098	.106
SELF	.020	.018	.023	.047	.058	.019
HEALTH	2.105	2.162	2.051	1.591	1.519	1.761
LIKE	.772	.820	.726	1.022	1.028	1.006
HUSHEALTH	.126	.257	—	.166	.236	—
HUSHAS						
$X = 62$	.132	.269	—	.185	.263	—
$X = 65$	.211	.431	—	.350	.497	—
HUSMAY						
$X = 62$	.079	.162	—	.165	.234	—
$X = 65$	.029	.060	—	.092	.130	—
HUSLATE	.038	.078	—	.101	.144	—
NMAR	.512	—	—	.296	—	—
RETBEF62	.263	.335	.194	.302	.360	.165
RETBEF65	.579	.653	.509	.584	.640	.452

Table 8A–2
Means of Variables Used in Regression Analysis: White Women, Aged 55–59

EARN82 ($1,000s)	11.7
ELINOW	
$X = 62$	.202
$X = 65$	.372
ELILAT	
$X = 62$	.282
$X \times 65$	.112

Table 8A–2 (continued)

PENAMT ($100,000s)	
X = 62	.753
X = 65	
ADDBEN ($100,000s)	
X = 62	.568
X = 65	
ASSETS	.362
HEALTH	2.135
HUSHEALTH	.240
NMAR	.369
RETBEF62	.170
RETBEF65	.561

Notes

1. This figure is a rough estimate calculated by weighting the incidence of pension receipt by different types of families and unrelated individuals by the proportion of women age 65 and over reporting each type of living arrangement (U.S. Bureau of the Census, 1985b, Table 34 and 1985a, Table 15).

2. A small number of women who do not know whether they will be eligible for a pension are included in the omitted category. In preliminary analyses these women were included in a separate category, but the coefficient for this category was never significantly different from the omitted group with no pension.

3. The discount rate used was 5 percent. Pension plans differ greatly in the extent to which benefits are reduced if early retirement is taken and in the extent to which larger benefits are offered if retirement is postponed beyond the normal retirement age offered by the plan. Kotlikoff and Smith (1983) report that nearly half of private employer plans with normal retirement at age 65 nevertheless offer unreduced benefits at age 62. Other plans reduce benefits for each year before normal retirement age, but typically by amounts that would not produce an actuarially fair benefit—thus offering an incentive for early retirement. In the calculation of ADDBEN and PENAMT no adjustment was made for reduced benefits for early retirement. For many people, PENAMT will thus be somewhat overestimated and ADDBEN underestimated. In the absence of information on individual plans, correct adjustment cannot be made. ADDBEN measures the effect of first becoming eligible better than the effect of additional years of work after eligibility is reached.

4. For more detail on the health measure see the description of the physical limitations and symptoms questions in notes 4 and 5, chapter 6. In the present analysis physical limitations and symptoms have been combined into one index.

5. Regressions using actual assets were also run, but did not show significant asset effects. Because sample sizes were greatly reduced due to missing data on assets, the regressions using the asset dummy were retained for the analyses reported here.

References

Anderson, K.; Clark, R.L.; and Johnson, T. 1980. Retirement in Dual Career Families." In R.L. Clark, ed., *Retirement Policy in an Aging Society.* Durham, N.C.: Duke University Press.

Clark, R.L.; Johnson, T.; and McDermed, A.A. 1980. "Allocation of Time and Resources by Married Couples Approaching Retirement." *Social Security Bulletin* 43:3-6.

Hall, A., and Johnson, T.R. 1980. "The Determinants of Planned Retirement Age." *Industrial and Labor Relations Review* 33:241-254.

Henretta, T.C., and O'Rand, A.M. 1980. "Labor Force Participation of Older Married Women." *Social Security Bulletin* 43:10-16.

———. 1983. "Joint Retirement in the Dual Worker Family." *Social Forces* 62: 504-520

Iams, H.M. 1985. "Characteristics of the Longest Job for New Retired Workers: Findings from the New Beneficiary Survey." *Social Security Bulletin* 48:5-21.

Kotlikoff, Laurence, J., and Daniel E. Smith. 1983. *Pensions in the American Economy.* Chicago: University of Chicago Press.

Morgan, J.N. 1980. "Retirement in Prospect and Retrospect." In G.T. Duncan and J.N. Morgan, eds., *Five Thousand American Families—Patterns of Economic Progress.* Vol. 8. Ann Arbor: Institute for Social Research, University of Michigan.

O'Rand, A.M., and Henretta, J.C. 1982. "Delayed Career Entry, Industrial Pension Structure, and Early Retirement in a Cohort of Unmarried Women." *American Sociological Review* 47:365-373.

Parnes, H.S., and Nestel, G. 1974. "Early Retirement." In H.S. Parnes et al., *The Pre-Retirement Years.* Vol. 4. Columbus, OH: Center for Human Resource Research, The Ohio State University.

Shaw, L.B. 1984. "Retirement Plans of Middle-Aged Women." *Gerontologist* 24: 154-159.

Shaw, L.B., and Gagen, M.G. 1984. "Retirement Decisions of Husbands and Wives." Special report to the U.S. Department of Labor. Columbus, OH: Center for Human Resource Research, The Ohio State University, 1984.

U.S. Bureau of the Census. 1985a. Current Population Reports, Series P-60, No. 147. *Characteristics of the Population below the Poverty Level: 1983.* Washington, D.C.: U.S. Government Printing Office.

U.S. Bureau of the Census. 1985b. Current Population Reports, Series P-60, No. 146. *Money Income of Households, Families, and Persons in the United States: 1983.* Washington, D.C.: U.S. Government Printing Office.

Index

About the Contributors

Ronald D'Amico is a consultant at SRI International in Menlo Park, California. Dr. Amico has published articles related to dual labor market theory, the career development of young men, and the consequences and determinants of the social organization and the labor market. His academic training is in sociology.

Mary Gagen is an assistant professor of Economics at the University of Toledo. She was a research associate with the National Longitudinal Surveys at the Center for Human Resource Research from 1977 to 1985 and she has contributed chapters to several NLS research volumes.

Robert J. Gitter is an associate professor of economics at Ohio Wesleyan University. He served as a visiting senior research associate at the Center for Human Resource Research in 1984–1985. He has published extensively on labor supply and apprenticeship training.

Donald R. Haurin, is an associate professor of economics at The Ohio State University. He has studied the spatial structure of cities, the provision of public services by local governments, migration, labor supply and changes in the distribution of income in the United States. A recent project studied changes in the quality of life in urban and rural areas of the midwest in the nineteenth century by relating the quality of life to public services, human height, and the distribution of wealth.

William R. Morgan, research scientist at the Center for Human Resource Research, was visiting associate professor in sociology at the University of Illinois, Chicago, in 1986. He has worked for the past five years on the National Longitudinal Surveys and Quality of Work Life projects at The Ohio State University. His articles on educational policy have appeared in *American Journal of Sociology, Sociology of Education, American Sociological Review,* and *Social Psychology Quarterly.*

Frank L. Mott holds a Ph.D. in Sociology from Brown University. He is a senior research scientist at The Ohio State University Center for Human Resource Research and associate project director of the National Longitudinal Surveys. He has worked with these data since 1975. He is principal author of two volumes about the young women's cohort: *The Employment Revolution* (MIT, 1982) and *Women, Work and Family* (Lexington Books, D.C. Heath and Company, 1978).

Elizabeth Peters received her Ph.D. from the University of Chicago. She is assistant professor of economics and research associate in the Program on Population Process in the Institute of Behavioral Sciences at the University of Colorado. She has done work on the economic consequences of divorce and has studied the effect of divorce laws on divorce rates and property settlements.